W9-ABI-002

from
Walter Rielly
August 12, 1947.

BY THE SAME AUTHOR

Uniform with this Volume

THE CROWN OF SORROW

THE MEANING OF LIFE

THE PRINCE OF PEACE

THE SCHOOL OF LOVE

JESUS CHRIST THE SON OF GOD

JESUS CHRIST
THE SON OF GOD

BY THE
MOST REV. ALBAN GOODIER, S.J.
ARCHBISHOP OF HIERAPOLIS

FIRST AMERICAN EDITION

BY SPECIAL ARRANGEMENT WITH
BURNS OATES & WASHBOURNE LTD.
PUBLISHERS TO THE HOLY SEE

GRAIL PUBLICATION

2329G

Nihil Obstat.

     INNOCENTIUS APAP, O.P.
         Censor Deputatus.

Imprimatur.

     EDM. CAN. SURMONT.
         Vicarius Generalis.

Westmonasterii,

     Die 2 Januarii, 1920.

Copyright 1947 by
St. Meinrad's Abbey, Inc.

CONTENTS

Part I

BELIEF IN JESUS CHRIST

Part II

THE HISTORIC CHRIST

CONTENTS

Part III

THE JUDGMENTS OF CHRIST

JESUS CHRIST THE SON OF GOD

THE PERSON OF JESUS CHRIST

"This child is set for the fall and for the resurrection of many in Israel, and for a sign which shall be contradicted."—Luke ii. 34.

A CHRISTIAN is one who not merely believes in Jesus Christ, but believes that Jesus Christ was and is actually God. It may seem to unbelievers an extravagance; to many it may appear arrogant; "to the Jews a stumbling-block, and to the Gentiles folly"; nevertheless the Christian does not flinch; he distinguishes his Master from every other, and he knows not only that he believes, but that he has grounds for his belief which compel the acceptance of everyone who really understands. Jesus Christ is truly God, at the same time that, and in the same measure that, He is truly man; upon that truth the whole of Christianity has been built.

In this whole-hearted acceptance, then, does Christianity separate itself from every other

1

faith. It does not make much of Jesus Christ because He was a great Master, because He developed some epoch-making moral code, because He wrote some book; Jesus Christ wrote no book. It does not honor Him as the greatest reformer of His nation; Christians belong to every nation, most do not belong to the nation of Christ, by His own people He was rejected. Nor is His Name to the true Christian a memory and no more; His life is not merely a fact of past history, a record of long ages past, preserved by some lasting monument; to the Christian Jesus Christ lives still, as really and truly as when He trod the streets of Nazareth, as when He ate and drank amongst men; to the Christian "he dieth now no more"; to him He is "yesterday, today, and the same for ever."

This obstinate fact of Jesus Christ, and of the Christian's faith in Jesus Christ, the Son of Man, the Son of God, has withstood every test, every opposition. It is as fresh today as when His follower first declared: "Thou art the Christ, the Son of the living God!" as when another follower, with his hand in His opened side, knelt before Him and exclaimed: "My Lord and my God!" The personality of Christ, that utter truthfulness which belongs to God alone, has survived in all its vigor, while all that would give it the lie has perished. He was re-

2

jected by His own, yet they are gone and He remains; excommunicated, yet His temple stands, and of theirs "not a stone is left upon a stone"; condemned and crucified, yet His Cross has become the glory of the world; His own were and are but weakling, yet from Him they have learned to "rejoice that they are accounted worthy to suffer something for the name of Christ."

As it was with Him in His day, so has it been with Him in every day since; always, as the prophet foretold, as He Himself foretold, He has been "a sign which shall be contradicted"; and yet always, with a vigor which has never waned, nay increasing in area with every generation, the belief in Jesus Christ, Son of Man, Son of God, has lived on. Religion has denied, and has closed up its ears against the seeming blasphemy; has done to death by millions those who proclaimed the belief; it has not stopped the torrent. Science has ridiculed; has "proved" the absurdity of this belief; the belief is as virile as ever. Philosophy has pondered, and has stood still before this "stumbling-block"; it has made no difference. Criticism has examined; has shown this Christ to be a myth, His followers to have been but madmen; criticism has destroyed itself, and the fact of Christ, Son of Man, Son of God, has emerged again from the cloud

3

of dust that had been created. Ignorance has roared with laughter and He has survived; false praise has flattered, has placed Him on the pinnacle of the temple, has offered the whole world to be His kingdom if He would but forgo that last title; Jesus Christ, Son of Man, Son of God, has passed all this by, and wins the world by His own weapons, in spite of every temptation to win it by surrender.

All this is matter of fact which the most unlettered may discover and test for himself; when men say that Christianity is waning they know not what they say. They will point to one single man in whom the faith is dead; they shut their eyes to the millions in whom it is as their life's blood. They will show on the map this spot where it appears to have lost its vitality, another where its fruits are said to be evil; they will not look the whole world round, and see this mighty tree spreading ever farther its branches, until the whole world is coming beneath its shade, towering as ever, fresh and green and fruitful, despite the dead leaves and withered twigs that from time to time gather round its root.

When we look back and ask ourselves upon what all this is built, from what it has come, who was this Jesus Christ in whom Christians

4

believe even unto death, the paradox is greater than ever. This man who emerged from a despised upland village, with no special training, no special experience of the ways and minds of men, who wrote no book, founded no school of thought, stirred no national movement, used no weapon for His conquest, raised no monument that His memory or His words might be remembered, who in nothing that He did can be classified with the other great reformers of the world—this is the man that has awakened all the ages, whose memory lives as does no other, whose vitality today is alive, while that of all others is dead, living only in the books they have written or the monuments they have left behind them.

Criticism has studied the phenomenon and has sought for an explanation. To quote its conclusions, its theories to solve the riddle of the facts, serves no useful purpose; one after another they have been set aside, criticism itself has discarded them as worthless. Then it has turned to seek for the solution in the Man Himself; and step by step it has risen to a grand confession. That Jesus Christ lived, it says, no man can doubt; that He was what history records Him, that too is absolutely certain.

And what does history record of Him? Criticism has looked again, and it has confessed His utter greatness; it has looked a third time, and it has declared that He is demonstrably the greatest Man that this world has seen. Again it has looked and has acknowledged that the greatness of this Man in unlike that of any other; it is a greatness all-including, all-transcending; it is unique, the like of Him was never seen before, and will never be seen again; it is a greatness greater than belongs to mere man. This Jesus Christ, it says, must have been more than man; in Himself, in His personality, in His influence, in His effects, there is that about Him which is more than human; in some sense He is divine.

So far has criticism gone; criticism that has had no heart for this conclusion, that had some far different end in view when it set out upon its researches. The Christian watches the development, and wonders why criticism has chosen to stop there. If Jesus Christ is all this, if He is unblemished truth, then He is more than this also, for He has declared Himself to be very God. History records it, in language and with evidence that only ignorance can venture to deny; even His enemies confess it in spite of themselves. Reason, the first of human guides, is driven to accept it; its only escape is to de-

6

clare beforehand that Jesus Christ, Man and God, is a thing which cannot, shall not be.

And last of all, deep down in the heart of every man there is a wistful longing to which this fact of Christ, truly Man and truly God, appeals with superhuman force. In the heart of everyone of us, if we will listen to it, there is a voice crying out: "Oh! that it might be so! That God might come to man, in order that man might be one with God!" It is not St. Paul alone that pities man for this unceasing craving; nor St. Augustine alone that, on this very account, declares man to be "naturally Christian"; there is something in us all which confesses that this fact of Jesus Christ, Son of Man and Son of God, at once human and divine, uniting God and Man in Himself, wholly above nature and above comprehension as it is, is also wholly consonant with human nature.

No; the Christian does no foolish thing, he lives in no dreamland, he follows no shadow, when he adopts the name of Jesus Christ, and puts his faith in Him and sets Him up for his ideal. He knows that he is right, that fact, and reason, and human nature are with him; and for those who do not see with him he can only feel compassion. With most it is only that they do not know; and for those with his Master he can pray: "Father, they know not!" With some it is that they will not; and for these, again with his Master, he can only lament and mourn. With a few—please God with a very few—it is malice that "will not serve"; and for these the Christian bears in mind that to the end his Lord shall be "a sign to be contradicted," but that in spite of all He is Master, and "of his kingdom there shall be no end."

THE CLAIM OF JESUS CHRIST

"These things are written that you may believe that Jesus is the Christ, the Son of God."—John xx. 31.

STUDENTS of the Gospels, of whatever school of belief, agree in accepting the first three, those of St. Matthew, St. Mark, and St. Luke, as quite genuine and authentic; on that point, they tell us, there can never again be any further question. But about the fourth Gospel, that of St. John, they are not agreed: its language, they say, is of a totally different kind, its method of thought belongs to different surroundings, external evidence shows that it was written long after the others, and probably not by the hand of St. John the Apostle at all. It is of little avail that these critics have, even among themselves, had their arguments and "proofs" broken to pieces one by one; it matters little that the vast majority of scholars uphold the genuineness of this Gospel no less than of the others; its enemies cling to the constantly repeated statement that the Gospel is not authentic, assuming it as proved, and declining to reopen the discussion.

The reason is not far to seek; for to put St. John's Gospel on the same footing as the others would be to involve themselves in unpalatable conclusions. The other Gospels lay down no thesis; they seem to aim at nothing more than depicting the Man Jesus Christ, as He has revealed Himself in word and action; what further conclusions are to be drawn may, think the critics, be considered matter of controversy. But with St. John it is different; from beginning to end he is clearly intending to prove a point; at the outset he identifies Jesus with the "Word," the Second Person of the Blessed Trinity; again and again he comes back upon it; at the end he concludes explicitly: "These things are written that you may believe that Jesus is the Christ, the Son of God." There can be no doubt about the matter: whatever we may hold on the teaching of the other Gospels, St. John leaves no room for question; accept him as authentic, and we must accept that a believer in the Gospels must also believe that Jesus Christ is truly God.

But this conclusion criticism will not accept. Has it not, it asks, already conceded enough? Has it not granted that Christ was the greatest man the world has ever known or will know?

That He is unique among men, in some sense too great to be a mere man? That in some mysterious way He was divine, specially inspired by the Godhead? What need to push the matter further? Above all in that uncompromising, merciless way employed by the author of the Fourth Gospel and the corresponding Epistles? Listen to his words:

"Who is a liar, but he who denieth that Jesus is the Christ? This is Antichrist, who denie[th] the Father and the Son. Whosoever denieth [the] Son, the same hath not the Father. He [that] confesseth the Son hath the Father also."

And again:

"We have seen and do testify that the F[ather] hath sent his Son to be the Savior of the w[orld] Whosoever shall confess that Jesus is th[e Son] of God, God abideth in him, and he in G[od."

And yet again:

"If we receive the testimony of me[n, the] testimony of God is greater. For this [is the] testimony of God, which is greater, beca[use he] hath testified of his Son. He that believeth in the Son of God hath the testimony of God in himself. He that believeth not the Son maketh himself a liar: because he believeth not in the testimony which God hath testified of his Son."

11

Such language is unendurable; it is unlike Him who was "meek and humble of heart"; very unlike one who could call himself with truth "the disciple whom Jesus loved"; therefore must criticism use its best endeavor to call the work spurious. It matters not that the evidence against it is of the very thinnest; in a law court, before unbiased judges, contrasted with the evidence on the other side it would scarcely be considered; still the point must be made, the position assumed, and so the last conclusion avoided.

But the Claim of Christ is not contained in the Gospel of St. John alone. It is contained in St. Matthew, St. Mark, and St. Luke; in St. Paul and the Acts of the Apostles; in the Old Testament and in the New; above all in the Life and Person of Jesus Christ Himself; whatever other title and honor He rejected, He did not reject the title of the Son of God, He did not refuse allegiance which only God might justly claim.

Yet this much may be granted; though the claim of Jesus Christ to be God cannot be mistaken, still it is less in word than in deed that it is maintained. He came among a stiff-necked people; in His gentle manner, He, who "would not break a bruised reed and smoking flax would not extinguish," would neither be merciless in His teaching. They looked for a Messiah; He would first prove to them that it was He. They watched for a new Lawgiver; He won them to Him by His new Law, and the way He delivered it: "I say to you," He said, and they recognized Him as "greater than Moses," "with authority greater than that of the Scribes." He "spoke as no man spoke," He did wonders such as no man did; and when they marvelled, and broke out in enthusiastic praise, He assured them that there was more behind, that He had greater things than this to teach them.

From wonders that belong to this creation He passed on to others. Not only did He make "the blind to see and the deaf to hear"; He took it upon Himself to forgive the sins of men. "Who is this that forgives sins?" men asked; they already understood the tremendous significance of that claim. And when at length one man ventured, and made that first act of faith in Him, and declared Him to be in truth "the Christ, the Son of the living God," he was answered with no rebuke, he was not corrected for his extravagance as on many another occasion; but he was blessed for that word, he was given an assurance that he had spoken nothing but the truth, and for the courage of his faith he

13

was raised to the highest honor given to man on this earth.

Once only do we find Him claiming the title in express terms; and that was at the crisis of His life. He stood before His judges; they had decided that He should die; the witnesses were called, but they did not agree, and there was danger that even sufficient show of reason might be wanting. At last the judge put a question; that question alone proves that he knew to what His prisoner laid claim. "I adjure thee," he said, "by the living God, that thou tell us if thou be Christ the Son of God." And the answer was no less explicit. "Jesus saith to him: Thou hast said it. Nevertheless I say to you, hereafter you shall see the Son of Man sitting at the right hand of the power of God and coming in the clouds of heaven."

The words were clear; the claim in set terms had at length been forced from Him before them all; and that it was understood in its literal and fullest sense the action of His judges shows. "Then the high priest rent his garments, saying: He hath blasphemed. What further need have we of witnesses? Behold, now you have heard the blasphemy. What think you? But they answering, said: He is guilty of death."

14

The blasphemy! Guilty of death! But there would be no "blasphemy" if the title "Son of God" were not to be taken literally; if in other words the claimant to the title did not claim to be in nature the same as God the Father Himself. It is not then St. John only that records the sentence: "According to our law he ought to die because he made himself the Son of God"; it is here contained in St. Matthew; on the evidence of all the Gospels He was put to death because He claimed to be very God. His disciple had acknowledged the claim, and He had honored him for it: His enemies had charged Him with accepting it, and He died for pleading guilty of the charge.

Can there be a middle course? Is it possible that this man Jesus Christ, the greatest man the world has seen, the most spotless, the most truthful; whose greatness, spotlessness, and truthfulness place Him above the range of manhood; who is "in some sense divine" in His sublimity; can it be that He should on this one point have been false, or mad, or eaten up with incontinent pride? The thought is not to be endured; if that could be so, then away for ever with all man's trust in man. Jesus Christ was not mad; He was not proud; He was not false. Jesus Christ was the greatest of men; His word

15

was utterly reliable; His life and person were witness to the truth of His word. And Jesus Christ claimed to be very God! We must take Him whole and entire, or we must take Him not at all.

And yet the middle course is taken by so many. The facts are there; accept them and the conclusion cannot be denied. But human nature has countless subterfuges; there is nothing that it cannot call into question if it will. "And some believed the things that were said: but some believed not. And when they agreed not among themselves they departed, Paul speaking this one word: Well did the Holy Ghost speak to our fathers by Isaias the prophet, saying: Go to this people and say to them: With the ear you shall hear and shall not understand; and seeing you shall see and shall not perceive. For the heart of this people is grown gross, and with their ears have they heard heavily, and their eyes they have shut, lest perhaps they should see with their eyes and hear with their ears and understand with their heart, and should be converted: and I should heal them."

THE FOLLOWING
OF JESUS CHRIST

*"The Pharisees therefore said among themselves:
Do you see that we prevail nothing? For behold
the whole world is gone after him."—John xii. 19.*

JESUS CHRIST has been acknowledged, even by
His enemies, to be the greatest and the truest
man this world has ever seen; He has been
acknowledged to be unique among men, too great
to be a mere man; in some sense, they say, He
is divine. And Jesus Christ has Himself gone
farther than this. Relying on His transparent
truthfulness as a foundation, on His life and its
wonderful content as a confirmation, on the
evidence of facts as a final proof, He has declared
Himself to be the Messias, the Redeemer for
which all the world, and especially the Jewish
world, was looking; He has made Himself the
fulfilment of prophecy and type contained in
Jewish history, the King, the Priest, the Prophet
that was to come, and has in Himself completed
and rounded off the Scripture; last of all, and
most stupendous of all, He has declared Himself

to be the Son of God, equal to God the Father, truly God even as He is truly man, and He has sealed this declaration with His blood.

So much in brief we have already seen, when considering the Person and the Claim of Jesus Christ. But, as He said on more than one occasion, He came into this world not for Himself only; He came "not to seek his own glory"; so far as He Himself was concerned, He was willing to remain "only Jesus," the "meek and humble of heart," who "would not break the bruised reed, and the smoking flax would not extinguish." He came for man, and for the good of man; He came, as He said, "for the lost sheep of the house of Israel," that men "might have life, and might have it more abundantly"; "For this I was born, and for this came I into the world, that I might give testimony to the truth. Everyone that is of the truth heareth my voice."

And Jesus Christ "knew what was in man," this man for whom He had come. It is in the nature of man that he should aspire to better things; it has always been so, it will be so to the end; no matter what his condition, prosperous or what is called unfortunate, there will always be something to improve, something to desire, something to rouse his heart to higher things. With himself man is seldom satisfied;

18

much more seldom is he satisfied with his surroundings. He has progress and improvement ever on his lips; schemes for the betterment of himself and his condition ever in his heart; man may be defined as the hungry-hearted creature of this world, whose life is for ever being torn asunder between high aspirations kindling noble efforts, and deep disillusionment prompting to despair.

For in spite of his desires and seeking for light, man for the most part gropes his way in darkness. He has his ideals, but he is not sure that his ideals make for the best; often enough, even when they are attained, he discovers he has made a mistake, and conquest does but emphasize his failure. Always and in almost everything he is in need of guidance, of example, of a standard by which he may live, and work, and build; and alongside of his effort he is to be ever found seeking for the lodestar about him. He seeks for it in books and in the written experience of men who have gone before him. He studies men of genius, "great" men as they are called, who have written their names across the pages of history, and hopes to find in them the means by which he can make his own life sublime. He searches into material things, twists matter this way and that, brings the whole of nature and nature's forces beneath his yoke, in the hope that this way he may be satisfied. And the answer is always the same; he still abides in darkness, he remains doubtful of his way, he still stands hesitating between truth and falsehood, life to him is still a vague riddle which he cannot solve.

Into the midst of all this gloom, once and once only in the history of man, has a man stepped with authority and declared that He in Himself was the solution. "I am the Way, the Truth, and the Life," He said boldly before all the world. "I am the Good Shepherd," He said to sinners; to others: "I am the door of the fold"; to those who had ears to hear: "I am the bread of life ... If any man eat of this bread, he shall live for ever: and the bread that I will give is my flesh for the life of the world."

Such was His astounding description of Himself; and He did not hesitate to crown all this by setting Himself up as an example for all men to follow. "Come to me," He said, "all you that labor and are burdened, and I will refresh you. Take up my yoke upon you, and learn of me, because I am meek and humble of heart: and you shall find rest to your souls. For my yoke is sweet and my burden light." And again on another occasion: "I have given you an example, that as I have done to you, so you do also." He called good men and bad; good women and women of evil fame; it seemed to matter little to Him who people were if only they would come and follow. "If any man thirst, let him come to me and drink!" This was the constant cry of this hungry-hearted Leader.

And yet this coming to Him was to be no child's play; He would refresh those who came, but they were to pay the price. To one who was attracted He said, without softening His words: "If thou wilt be perfect, go sell what thou hast, and give to the poor, and thou shalt have treasure in heaven: and come, follow me"; and again to many in general: "If any man will come after me let him deny himself and take up his cross daily and follow me." Nor was He afraid of warning. "He that is not with me is against me, and he that gathereth not with me scattereth"; and again: "He that shall be ashamed of me and of my words, of him the Son of Man shall be ashamed, when he shall come in his majesty and that of his Father, and of the holy angels."

There is no mistaking language such as this. It is the language of Him who was described by His friends as He who "spoke as one having authority, and not as the Scribes," and of whom even His enemies, come to catch Him in His speech, said: "Did ever any man speak as this man hath spoken?" Did any indeed? For it was not so much the doctrine that He taught that impressed them; it was the unhesitating emphasis on His own Personality. Other men had uttered great things; they had taught high moral doctrines, they had written deep books, they had founded schools of thought, and philosophy, and moral, and even of religion; and men were content to ponder their words through every generation, even when their author had been buried in the past or wrapped about with the mists of mythology. But it was not so with Jesus Christ; He wrote no book, He belonged to and founded no school, He "came not to destroy, but to perfect"; it was Himself and not merely His word, His own Person and not so much His teaching, that was "the way, the truth, and the life," the secret of regeneration for all mankind.

And as He taught Himself as the new principle of life, so He taught the following of Himself as the secret of man's true progress. "Meek and humble of heart" as He certainly was, yet He dared to claim this high position. Daring and arrogant as it might well be thought, yet He could boldly ask in defiance: "Which of you shall accuse me of sin?" Hard and unbending as His following was shown to be, yet His enemies had to confess in dismay: "Behold all the world goes after him."

Nor was He misunderstood by those who followed. It may be that in the Scriptures, in the New Testament and in the Epistles, the actual doctrine of Christ Our Lord on some special point is not always clear to the ordinary reader; in this, as in all else where knowledge looks to be accurate, the scholar and specialist are needed for its interpretation. But of one thing there can be no doubt whatsoever; what Jesus Christ said of Himself as the beginning and the end, before all doctrine and all practice, that His followers took up and emphasized without palliation. "Sanctify the Lord Christ in your hearts," says St. Peter; this is his standard of life. "Grow in grace, and in the knowledge of Our Lord and Saviour Jesus Christ," he says in another place; this is his standard of knowledge. St. Paul: "I judged not myself to know anything among you, but Jesus Christ, and him crucified"; and for practice: "Be ye followers of me, as I am of Christ." Last of all, as though he could say no more: "The end of the law is Christ."

We listen to all this, and we are driven back on all that we have said before. Without any doubt this Jesus Christ is of two things one; either Christ and Christianity are the greatest fraud, founded on the greatest arrogance, that have ever been imposed upon mankind, or they stand alone, unique and supreme and without any parallel, among the great regenerating influences of this world. But they are not the first; their greatest enemies will not accuse them of that. Then they are the second. Jesus Christ in Himself is the single Leader; to know Him is the truth, to follow Him is the way, to live by Him is the life; and to know Him, as what He claimed to be, the Son of God, to follow Him, to live by Him as such, that is what we mean by Christianity. Other things may come out of this, doctrines, practices, devotions, standards; but this is the essential. Says St. John, "We know that the Son of God is come: and he hath given us understanding that we may know the true God, and may be in his true Son. This is the true God, and life eternal."

THE REWARD OF JESUS CHRIST

"If any man love me, he will keep my word, and my Father will love him, and we will come to him, and will take up our abode in him."—John xiv. 23.

JESUS CHRIST was truly man, living among men, "in all things the same as man"; He was the greatest man this world has seen; in some mysterious sense He was more than mere man; in some sense He was divine; this much history and science have acknowledged. Jesus Christ claimed to be the Messiah, the foretold of all generations; He claimed to be the King that was to come, the Lord of all the world; He declared Himself to be the Son of God Himself, in the strictest sense of that term; He died for that declaration; but never has any one of His claims been disproved. Jesus Christ set Himself up as the Model according to which all humanity should be built, the Source from which humanity should draw its life, the Light by whose guidance humanity should reach its goal; in His lifetime His "arrogance" was not denounced, rather His authority was reverenced and feared; since His

25

time this leadership has been the ever growing secret of the world's rallying and progress.

Thus far we have already seen. But the significance of Christ does not stop here. Man's life is full of burden, and the burden of life does not diminish with what is called success or progress. No success is complete, no progress reaches its final goal; not only do the common burdens remain, sickness, and anxiety, and misunderstanding, and the rest, but success and progress themselves bring other burdens of their own. Man learns, even at his best, to be content with partial fruit; he accepts as inevitable a certain sense of failure; he submits to what he deems the inevitable, and is content if on the whole the satisfactions outweigh the disappointments; he trains himself to a lower level than his first ambitions pictured, and tells himself that this is enough; this, he sees, is all that can be hoped for in this life, and he conforms himself in accordance with his circumstances.

So have concluded many men in their own hearts, and most if not all the leaders of men have confirmed the conclusion. Only one has dared to come forward with a quite different solution, a quite other outlook; one which none could have put forward who had no commission from another world. He finds men laboring and heavily-burdened, and He says: "Come to me ... and I will refresh you." He finds them eager to do good to mankind, and He calls: "Come after me, and I will make you fishers of men." He finds them oppressed with poverty, with adversity, with suffering, and He gives them joy in their trouble: "Blessed are the poor in spirit, for theirs is the kingdom of heaven. Blessed are the meek, for they shall possess the land. Blessed are the mournful, for they shall be comforted. Blessed are they that suffer persecution for justice' sake, for theirs is the kingdom of heaven."

But He does not stop here. Not only does He teach man that to accept trial and suffering is to conquer it, but He flings about the blessings of this life with a lavish hand, and then crowns them all with the blessings of another. Let men but give up everything for Him, and the reward shall be overwhelming; let them but pour themselves out in generosity and they shall have an abundant return; let their lives bear upon them the stamp of charity and there shall await them a joy that "eye hath not seen, nor ear heard, neither hath it entered into the heart of man to conceive."—"Amen, I say to you, there is no man who hath left house, or brethren or sisters, or father, or mother, or children, or lands for my sake and for the gospel, who shall not receive an hundred times as much, now in this time; houses, and brethren, and sisters, and mothers, and children, and lands, with persecutions: and in the world to come life everlasting."—"Give, and it shall be given to you: good measure and pressed down and shaken together and running over shall they give into your bosom."—"Then shall the king say to them that shall be on his right hand: Come, ye blessed of my Father, possess you the kingdom prepared for you from the foundation of the world. For I was hungry, and you gave me to eat: I was thirsty, and you gave me to drink: I was a stranger, and you took me in: naked, and you covered me: sick, and you visited me: I was in prison, and you came to me."

Even yet He does not stop. Not only shall the good things of this world not be wanting to those who surrender all for Him, not only shall there be an assurance in the world to come, but, here and hereafter, there shall be a special joy, a special satisfaction, to be found in union with Himself. "He that eateth my flesh, and drinketh my blood, hath everlasting life: and I will raise him up at the last day."—"If anyone love me he will keep my word, and my Father will love him, and we will come to him, and will make our abode with him."—"If you abide in me, and my words abide in you, you shall ask whatever you will, and it shall be done to you."—"Peace I leave with you, my peace I give unto you; not as the world giveth, do I give unto you. Let not your heart be troubled, nor let it be afraid."

There is something tremendous in all this. It assumes a background which human thought cannot hope to fathom. His fellow-countrymen heard Him, learned and unlearned, they did not laugh at His assumption, they did not despise this self-appointed healer of the ills of man, they listened to His words with reverence, convinced in their hearts that they were dealing with that which was beyond themselves. Once or twice did some venture to ask: "Who is this?" and "How can this man do this?" But their very question showed that they had understood aright, and that, even though they would not believe, yet they did not scoff. But some believed, though they did but partly understand; and of these it is no wonder that history records, when He had passed away, that "they rejoiced that they were accounted worthy to suffer something for the name of Christ."

Nor has the lesson ever been forgotten, that saving lesson of joy in suffering, of laughter in the midst of tribulation, of the ultimate union with Him which makes all else seem as nothing, caught from the words of Jesus Christ, ringing loud in the pages of St. Paul, and echoed through the two thousand years that have followed since. The Cross of Christ is the symbol; the symbol of suffering, the symbol of charity, the symbol as well of heroism and glory; in it, and in the blending of these three about it, the promise of Jesus Christ has been and is being abundantly fulfilled. Beneath that symbol, and in the hope that it implies, how many millions have cheerfully "cast their bread upon the waters," given up all they had and all they were for His sake, and after a long time it has come back to them! Martyrs have suffered and died, apostles have given their lives in teaching, confessors have bound themselves to serve, hermits and anchorites have torn themselves from the way of men, virgins have renounced all that life holds as most seductive—the procession has gone on from the beginning, and has increased as it has moved forward; and whether we look back, or whether we look round us in the present with understanding eyes, we are compelled to confess that in its ranks, if anywhere in the world, is true contentment to be found. These are they who "have nothing and possess all things," the meek who still possess the land, the sufferers, it may be, but still the men and women whose sorrow is turned into joy.

But we need not look only to the heroes of Christ to discover the fulfilment of His promise; in the hearts of those around us, in our own hearts, it is easily discovered what it is to live with Him, and what it is to live without Him. Without Him, man is no further than he was two thousand years ago; there is the same burden to be borne, however changed the circumstances; the same effort to remove it, to lighten it, to shift it from one shoulder to another; in the end the same discovery that escaped it cannot be, and therefore the same grim determination to make the best of this curse of humankind. But with Him, how different! The burden is still there; He gave no promise that it should be removed; on the contrary, He foretold that it would abide, and for some would even be increased. But he has borne it first, and that has made all the difference. The Ideal Man among men has borne it, the Man most lovable of all the children of men, the Conqueror of all hearts, the Inspirer of all heroes, the Companion of all toilers, the Help of every wounded man; He has borne it, He has ennobled it, He has shown us that indeed suffering is worth while; more than that, He has made suffering golden, so that apart from anything that may come after, suffering becomes its own reward. No wonder there is joy of heart where Jesus Christ abides; that is the

31

first degree of His hundredfold even in the valley of this death: "Your sorrow shall be turned into joy."

"Who is this, for the winds and the sea obey Him?" Who indeed? Can He be other than that which He said He was, who commands not the winds and the sea alone, but the heavens and the earth, this world and the next, who "humbled himself, becoming obedient unto death, even to the death of the cross. For which cause God also hath exalted him, and hath given him a name which is above all names: that in the name of Jesus every knee should bow, of those that are in heaven, on earth, and under the earth; and that every tongue should confess that the Lord Jesus Christ is in the glory of God the Father."

CHRIST BEFORE CHRIST

It is scarcely possible for a student of antiquity
to get away from one characteristic which distinguishes it from our own time. In every generation, and under every civilization, it is true,
man is ever looking forward to something better;
he is for ever hoping that reform will be brought
about which will make all the difference to his
condition. But between the ancient and the modern interpretation of this hope there is all the
difference in the world; for while in our time man
takes it for granted that this reform must be
wrought by himself if at all, in ancient times
he seemed to expect that in some mysterious
way it would be wrought for him from without.

I say there is no mistaking this trait of antiquity, at all events in that section of it which
anticipated the civilization of the West; of the
East I am not competent to speak, though here,
too, I have heard scholars say that something

of the same is to be found. It is to be seen in
the religion of Greece, especially in such stories
as that of Prometheus, who stole fire from heav-
en to succour mankind, and was nailed to a rock
for his crime; in much of the craving of Greek
philosophy, which yearned for the millennium,
in which all things should be made anew, and
which only the gods could give. It is to be traced
in the mind of the Romans, material, legal,
unaspiring though they were; both in the occasional outbursts of their poets, remodelling old
traditions of the Light of the World that was to
come, and in the bent of their philosophy, which
clung to the hope, in spite of disappointment,
that somehow and sometime the new era would
be granted.

But pre-eminently was this true of one particular people that lived apart from all the rest.
Let us believe what we may of the Jewish race,
their origin, their traditions, their peculiar history, one thing about them is abundantly clear
and cannot be contested: they were for much
more than a thousand years a nation separated
from the world, they possessed a faith in God
more single, more pure than can be found in any
other people; their standard of morality, whatever their practice, was more refined and exalted,
their law was a thing unique, and, most marked
of all, their faith, their national unity, their

34

ideals, one may say everything that distinguished them as Jews, was built up on the one idea, of an age that was to come, of a Person who was to be the Master of that age, and who was to be one of themselves. This was the dominating idea in the mind of every faithful Jew, loyalty to which was his first duty; he belonged to a chosen people, and from his people would one day come the Ruler, the Teacher, the Saviour of all mankind.

We speak of the Jewish Bible as if it were a single book; we forget that it is a collection of books, written during a period of more than a thousand years, an imperishable record of a people in its origin, in its development, and in its material decline. But one thing binds these books into a single whole; it is the thread that runs through them, unbroken by any vicissitude, or change of fortune, or disillusionment, proving that from first to last this people clung to the belief in "him that was to come." Round that thought their literature centered, upon it their law was built, in conformity with it their religious rites were elaborated; if one were asked in effect what the Bible contained, it might be answered that it is a record of the tradition of a Champion that was to come, and the way that tradition made and kept a people.

Of this there can be no doubt whatsoever. The Bible as history is an indubitable document, and there is no historian who calls this fact into question, explain it or deal with it as he may. But having secured this point we find we must go further. Not only among the Jews was the tradition of a coming Saviour of the world preserved pure and undefiled, and made the basis of all else, but this tradition in itself grew with advancing ages. There came men from time to time who added to this tradition; a word here, an interpretation there, at another time an orientation or point of view; in various ways, as the Jews were recalled to their fidelity, or reminded of the heirloom they possessed, they were taught with ever-growing clearness the nature of "him that was to come"—the King, the Priest, the Prophet of the future.

Nor was it only through these seers, the prophets as they were called, that the future Saviour was revealed; in many other ways and from many other sources the knowledge concerning Him was gathered up. Events took place in the history of this "chosen people," and they learned to interpret these events in the light of the future; somehow they were foreshadowings of that which was to happen. Ceremonies, and rites, and customs had been established among themselves; each of these had its significance with regard to the climax of them all. Great men arose among them, striking in some characteristic, fulfilling some particular purpose; not one of these but was studied as in some sense a type of Him in whom all greatness was to be gathered and completed.

Let us take but a few examples, a very few out of many. The Jews were for years exiles in Egypt; Egypt, then, was in some way to be a place of exile for the Great Deliverer. The slaying and eating of the Paschal Lamb, of which not a bone was to be broken, was the rite instituted as a remembrance of their deliverance; He, too, should in some way be slain and eaten, while not a bone of His body should be broken, as a sign of the deliverance of men. The manna fell from heaven to feed the wanderers in the desert; He, too, should bring down bread from heaven. Melchisedech, the priest who sacrificed in bread and wine alone, Moses, the giver of the Law, David, the meek King, yet the mighty founder of the throne, Elias, who fasted forty days—the Priest of the future would be "according to the order of Melchisedech," His Law would transcend that of Moses, as a king He would be humble and meek, though "of his kingdom there would be no end," He, too, would fast for forty days, as did the greatest of their prophets.

Thus from all sides did the tradition receive light, so much that its study and interpretation became a chief labor of those who may be called the theologians of the Jews. Generations before the prophecies were fulfilled the school of these theologians was at work, interpreting words and events, collating texts, calculating times and places and signs, high and low "looking for the redemption of Israel." A modern Jewish convert to Christ, steeped in the literature and history and traditions of his people, has set down more than five hundred texts of the Bible, taken from these writers alone, all bearing upon the one central figure; and he does not pretend that the list he gives is exhaustive.

What, then, did this people know of "him that was to come"? We cannot say all: it is enough if we state main outlines. He was to be born of woman; He was to be of the line of Abraham, of Isaac, of Jacob; lastly, and definitely, He was to belong to the royal house of David. He should be born in Bethlehem, and of a Virgin Mother; kings should come to venerate Him there, while for those who lived about there should be weeping and lamentation. He should go down to, and come out of Egypt; yet none the less He should be known as one from Nazareth. He should establish a new priesthood, whose sacrifice should be in bread and wine; He should work miracles among the people, should be their Good Shepherd, gentle and accessible to all, and yet their Lord and Master; and one day in token of this, He should come into the city "meek and riding on an ass," even while the people cried, "Hosanna to the son of David!"

And yet in the end He should be rejected. He should be the "man of sorrows," betrayed by His own and sold for thirty silver pieces. He should be taken and tried; false witness should be brought against Him; in spite of this He should be scourged, condemned, and crucified; His hands and feet should be dug with nails, the people should "look upon him whom they had pierced," yet not a bone of His body should be broken. He should be buried; and then, on the third day, in some mysterious manner, this King of life and death should come to His own. Then should be founded the kingdom, in which Gentile and Jew should rejoice; the Lord would "lead captivity captive," and ascend in triumph to His throne.

Such, in briefest outline, is what might have been known concerning Jesus Christ before Jesus Christ was born. Much, it is true, was not clearly understood; it could not have been understood until the promise was fulfilled. But after He was gone, when His messengers went out and explained the tradition, and showed its fulfilment in His life down to every detail, then by thousands they understood and believed; and upon that acceptance the foundations of Christianity were laid. This is a fact of history, documented at every turn; type, antitype, and the recognition of the fulfilment of the one in the other, by men who were competent to know.

Never before, never since, has such a strange thing occurred in human experience, that a man's life should be known long years before He was born; is it strange that when He did come He was able boldly to declare: "Before Abraham was, I am," and should claim for Himself all that such a declaration implied? "Thou art the Son of God, thou art the King of Israel," was the response of the "true Israelite in whom there was no guile."

THE SURROUNDINGS OF CHRIST

WE have seen what a vital part the Promise of the Redeemer played in the mentality of the Jews of old. It was their one rallying-cry in the midst of endless divisions, their one hope when everything else was desperate; come what might, this glory, of being the race from whom the Saviour of the world would come, would one day be theirs. In that expectation they lived on, around it they gathered signs that foretold Him; when the day did dawn there were many proofs in their hands by which He could be recognized.

All this is true; but here at once we are confronted with a problem. Though so much was known of Him beforehand, though even at the time of His coming men were specially awake to discover Him, still the fact remains that when He actually did come He was not recognized; more than that, when He produced His credentials He was rejected; even His friends, those who were continually about Him and knew Him best, did not fully understand His significance to the very end. "How long a time have I been

with you," He had to say to them, the last time
He was with them, "and you have not known
me!" How is this to be explained? How is it
that, with the evidence to us so manifest, with
no other rival claimant to dispute His right, with
no other explanation but Himself put forward to
solve the prophetic argument, nevertheless by
those who should have known best He was set
aside, and even put to death for His arrogant
assumption?

The question makes it clear that if we would
understand the historic Jesus Christ aright we
must understand something of His surroundings,
the circumstances and the people among which
He lived. For indeed they were a peculiar people,
cut off and markedly distinguished from the rest
of the world, in history, in character, and in
their actual condition. Long centuries before
they had migrated from Egypt into this "Land
of Promise," already a people apart; in this land
they had built themselves up, making their own
laws, observing their own customs, permanently
influenced in little or nothing by the nations
around them.

Yet they cannot be called a "holy" people; in
a sense they cannot even be called faithful. At
times they adopted strange gods among themselves; at times they looked hungrily out to the
ways and manners of others; their priests fell

42

away, false prophets were accepted; when men of truth rose up among them their chief cry was in denunciation of this "stiff-necked people," and they were punished with death for their courage. But the day of retribution came; Israel had undermined itself, it fell a prey to the northern invader, its people were carried away into captivity and scattered far and wide over a great empire; to the ordinary onlooker, even to the shrewd historian, it might well have been concluded that the people of the Jews had become extinct.

But it was far from being so. Generations later, when the ban upon them was removed, there wandered back to Jerusalem a paltry remnant, some 50,000 souls at the most, to build up again their nation and to rekindle its faith in itself, out of the ruins of the past. In the interval much had been lost; many traditions had perished, their rites and ceremonies had to be learned anew, worst of all, their very language had been forgotten, so that their sacred books were closed to all but the learned. But their faith had not been shaken, in spite of the years of subjection in Babylon; faith in the one God and Father, in Him that was to come, in themselves as chosen to give Him to the world.

Centuries followed, during which this little band increased and multiplied, from without and from within, in spite of foreign conquest and subjection, until once more the land of Palestine was also the land of the Jews. They fell in succession beneath the yoke of Persia, of Greece, and of Rome; each of these left its mark upon them; but the Jewish tradition remained, however affected in its details. Though foreign domination necessitated a foreign law, still the Jewish law stood untouched; more than that, there grew up around it lawyers and doctors, men who made it their profession to interpret it to the people, and to give it further applications as time went on.

But here was the beginning of misery; and it was fostered by other circumstances. The Law was there, perfect from the hand of Moses, ancient and sacred; but it soon became so "sanctified" that the spirit of the Law was lost, the letter only remained, and men were oppressed with untold burdens, by an ever-increasing worship of "the letter of the Law." Still it was too sacred to be changed; anathema to him who should venture to alter one tittle of this sacred inheritance. And in the Law much was included; the tradition of the kingdom, the tradition of the king, not least; and the times, and the circumstances of the times, had given the terms a new definition, and therefore the Law itself a new interpretation.

44

For were not they the "chosen people"? And had they not been protected from the beginning, set apart, educated, entrusted with the secret of the world? And while other kingdoms had passed away, had not their own lived on, however crushed, however mutilated? They were the children of Abraham, they were the followers of Moses, they were the subjects of the house of David, no matter what other house might be in temporary occupation. The house of David would again revive; out of it would one day come the One who would rule His people Israel; His kingdom should spread to the ends of the earth, and of it there should be no end; when He came in triumph, when He had reduced His enemies beneath His feet, then would men see the glory of Israel, the glory of the Lord.

So did the mind of the Jewish people close itself in upon itself, to the exclusion of all others. Their God was the God of Israel, who loved Israel above all, and would bring the rest of men to their subjection. Their law was the wording of morality; he who kept the law was good, he who did not keep, he who did not know it, was outcast and reprobate; and the vast Gentile world was included in the condemnation. Observance was better than motive, for this was the fulfilment of the law; as a man kept the law, so much merit did he earn in this life and the next; and once more the Gentile was proved to be of no account. Keep the law, develop the law, increase the obligations of the law, this was the mark of the faithful Jew; and the time would come when the greatest observer of the law would re-establish the kingdom of the law in the world. There were punctilious Pharisees to emphasize by word and example this domination of the law; Scribes and students, to interpret it in every detail, and make it binding on the people; Zealots, who gave it a political turn, and were ready to hail the king and kingdom the moment He should appear; ascetic Essenes, to spread over the law the halo of manifest sanctity; even opportunist Sadducees, to whom religion mattered nothing, but whose influence killed the truth of tradition, while it gave full rein to these false ideals.

Such was the prevalent attitude of mind among the leaders of the Jewish people. They still held the tradition, the prophecies were still known to them; but their eyes were blinded by mists of their own making, and they looked for "him that was to come" with an expectation very different from that which was to be. But it was not wholly so. Among the Jews at home in Palestine, even more among the thousands of Jews scattered throughout the world, this narrowed interpretation had not prevailed. It might

46

almost be said that the farther one receded from the center of Judaism, the more was the tradition untrammelled; so that, when the King did come, and when Jerusalem would have none of Him, He was received in Asia Minor, and Greece, and Rome, and even to this day He is received in the uttermost parts of the earth.

Perhaps, then, to explain the rejection of Jesus Christ by those who had looked for Him so long, and who had so many signs by which they might know Him when He came, is not so difficult. There was much that was known, but much that was unknown, much that was clear, but much that need sympathetic interpretation; much that might be borne in mind, and much that an unwilling mind might find it convenient to ignore. Times had been hard for this downtrodden people; and it was some relief to live upon hopes, however false and distorted. Religious pride had been fostered for centuries; and there is nothing so hard to break as religious pride, nothing which is at the same time so blinding. Ignorance had blinded the lowly, conceit had blinded those in high places; the result was, as Christ said when He came, that the blind led the blind until both fell into the ditch. They saw Him, but He was not according to their ideas. He came to them "meek and riding on an ass"; they looked for a Lord of the world. He spoke "as one having

47

authority"; they demanded one who submitted to the law, as they understood it. He made a claim for which they had no explanation; and the law said that one who claimed such a thing should be put to death. "We have a law, and according to that law he ought to die, because he made himself the Son of God."

THE LIFE OF CHRIST

WE have seen something of Jesus Christ as interpreted from the prophets; we have seen something of the circumstances and surroundings in which He lived and died, especially of those surroundings which were in opposition to His coming and His mission. The expectation of Him was alive and keen; but that He might be duly recognized, how much had to be corrected, how much to be unlearned!

Into the midst of these surroundings came Jesus Christ, from His hidden life in Galilee. He had no credentials but Himself and His own personality, no support from the world outside but man's instinctive reverence for truth and purity. He knew for what He had come; to teach Himself to men and to found among them that new kingdom which should have no end. But for this He must begin by correcting the current ideas of the kingdom. He must show men that His Kingdom was "not of this world"; that it was not to be marked by worldly wealth and worldly honors; that it was a "kingdom within,"

a kingdom in which the poor should be blessed
and the suffering, and should be possessed by
the meek and humble. This was a new thing
indeed, and those learned in the law looked
askance at this strange interpretation; from the
first it was clear in which quarter His greatest
opposition would be found.

But He knew from the beginning what was in
man, the good as well as the evil. That He
Himself would fail in the end He knew, for "so
it must be done"; but the seed that He would
sow must bear its fruit in season. He drew a
band of men about Him, the training of whom
was His one chief care; beyond these, by words
that human heart could not resist, by deeds that
filled men with wonder, He fascinated all that
would accept a little of His spirit. "A great
prophet has risen up among us, and God hath
visited his people," men began to cry; and they
reflected upon Him: "Behold he hath done all
things well; he hath made the deaf to hear, and
the dumb to speak." Of Himself, as yet, He
said little; at present it was enough that men
should learn to believe in Him, should have their
eyes opened to the grander vision of the grander
kingdom; when the soil had been prepared, then
would be the time for the high doctrines of the
new revelation to be taught.

Nevertheless, by slow degrees, the seed was being sown. He spoke "as one having authority," and men learned to bow before His word: He looked out on the world with a universal range, and the minds of His hearers were widened to include more than their little selves. His language was at once the simplest and the most sublime, such that both the lowliest might understand and the most learned might ponder with fruit till the end of time. "Never did any man speak as this man spoke," said even His silenced enemies. .

In setting such as this He told them of the Fatherhood of God, His Father and theirs, who was that and nothing else to the children who would take Him; of the kingdom He had come to found; of the members of that kingdom, the poor, the meek, the merciful, the clean of heart, the peacemakers; of the condition of entrance into the kingdom: "Unless you become as little children you shall not enter"; and then, by degrees there dawned out the teaching of the king, the Christ, the Son of David, the Son of Man, and lastly the very Son of the very God.

And while He so drew on His people that hearing they might hear and understand, He yielded to their weakness as human beings by working wonders among them. It was once the fashion for so-called scholarship to make light of this part of the life of Jesus, to pass the record over as the fruit of a latter-day enthusiasm and exaggeration. But scholarship today is more honest; it acknowledges that enthusiasm will not explain the undoubtedly authentic narrative; whatever we may think of Jesus Christ, the fact of His miracles is certain. He cured the diseases of those about Him, He raised their dead; He stilled the storm and He calmed the waves; He loosened tongues and cast out devils; and men whispered among themselves: "We have seen wonderful things today."—"When the Christ cometh, shall he do more miracles than those which this man doth?"

In this way, and by means such as these, did the opening career of Jesus Christ march forward to apparent triumph. But it received a sudden check. If He was the Christ, then was He the promised King that should lead His followers to victory; to the end they would not dismiss the craving for the "kingdom of this world" that lay deepest in their hearts. And while this weed still grew in the land, there was also growing the harvest; the climax of each came at once. They strove to "take him by force and make him king," and He would have none of it; on the very next day, when if ever He had their hearts in His hands, He spoke to them

52

of the "bread from heaven" which He had come to give them, the offer of His own body and blood, and it was too much. Be He who He might, this was after all not the kind of Christ for whom they had been prepared. It was easy now to find excuse. "The Jews, therefore, murmured at him because he had said, I am the living bread which came down from heaven. And they said, Is not this Jesus the son of Joseph, whose father and mother we know? How then saith he, I came down from heaven?"—"The Jews therefore strove among themselves, saying, How can this man give us his flesh to eat?"—"Many therefore of his disciples hearing it said, This saying is hard, and who can hear it?"—"After this, many of his disciples went back, and walked no more with him."

The zenith of His glory with the people had been reached. It was the moment for His great revelation. And they "would not." From that moment came the opportunity of the Pharisees and Scribes, who had hitherto labored in vain to belittle Him before the world. Henceforth for them it would be an easier matter, for their heart was no longer with Him. Still not all went away. Among His inner circle, the chosen band that was always with Him, the greater light had begun to dawn; and one of them had already anticipated the climax of His teaching by the

declaration: "Thou art the Christ, the Son of
the living God." On this inner circle He now
leaned; to it He spoke more and more in particular; He revealed to it His glory, and at the
same time His disappointed heart; in it He lived
at peace; without, for the remainder of His days
was heard little but storm and denunciation and
warning and the din of battle.

The evening of His day began to draw in, and
it was marked with many signs. If hitherto the
Life of Jesus had been one of labor, now the
labor was even more pronounced. "I must work
the works of him that sent me whilst it is day,"
He said; "The night cometh when no man can
work." He had much yet to teach, for He had
to put before His own the last lesson, the lesson
of Himself. Hitherto he had spoken mainly of
the kingdom; now He spoke of Himself the King,
of Himself the Bread of Life, of Himself the
Living Water, the Light of the World, the Good
Shepherd, the Door of the Fold, the Resurrection
and the Life, the Master and Lord, who nevertheless proved His mastership by service. And
to the outer world, by contrast, He emphasized
Himself in many other ways. He was the stone
that had been rejected, the prophet that had been
contemned, but the day would soon come when
they would find Him the Judge of the living
and the dead.

At last came the end. He was prepared, and He had prepared His own, for the final tragedy. Then He went up boldly to the scene of His rejection. The people still wondered; had He but yielded a little to their craving for a world-king, what might not have come of that triumphant entry into the city on the first Palm Sunday! But He would be true to Himself; and the Pharisees probed Him with their subtleties, the Sadducees with their mocking questions, till the minds of men were confused and despondent. The time had come; the door was opened by a traitor; and Jesus Christ yielded to "their hour and the power of darkness," yet to the end in a strange way master of Himself and of His very executioners. "He was offered because he willed it"; the "prophecy of the Scriptures" had to be fulfilled; in this was the unity of His life perfected.

Such in brief is an outline of the Life of Jesus Christ as cold history seems to teach it to us, and as the hardest unbeliever will freely recognize it. He came as Man, "in all things like to man, sin alone excepted," and He submitted to the storm of life into which His lot was thrown. "He did all things well"; "because of his good works" His enemies "accused him not"; He gave Himself to others, He did nothing for Himself. He came "a light into the world," but He did not force Himself upon men. They "loved the darkness better than the light," and He submitted to His lot. And when we look upon the whole, and the shadow of the Cross that lies upon it, we see how befitting it is that He should so identify Himself with this aspect of humanity. His death no less than His life dragged out the confession from an onlooker: "Of a truth this was the Son of God."

THE CHARACTER OF CHRIST

WE have seen how the prophecies concerning Jesus Christ were marvellously fulfilled in the details of His life. But there was another content of those prophecies that is still more striking; for from them we may gather not only what He was to be and do, but also the kind of man He was to show Himself. And the chief characteristic of these prophecies is their apparent contradiction; so opposite are they that men might well give up the attempt to fit them together; this Saviour who nevertheless should fail; this commanding and stern authority, whose wand would be in His hand to sift the chaff from the grain, and yet who would be so meek, and humble, and forgiving, that He would not break the bruised reed, and smoking flax would not extinguish; this "Wonderful, Counsellor, God the mighty, Father of the world to come, Prince of Peace," and yet with "no beauty in him, nor comeliness, despised and the most abject of men, a man of sorrows, and acquainted with infirmity."

Nevertheless, when He did appear among men, how more than completely did He harmonize in

Himself these strange opposites! Indeed, for one who knows human nature, it is this very fact which places Him, even in the light of history alone, pre-eminent among the sons of men. Other men possess the weakness of their greatness; to be endowed with one high quality almost of necessity implies the lack of another; few men are two things at once, much less are opposite things at once, none are at once perfect in every part; as the proverb tells us, "The highest mountains cast the deepest shadows." Jesus Christ, alone among men, can be found wanting in nothing. His enemies looked for a flaw and acknowledged they found none; students since have been baffled in the effort to reduce Him to the ordinary category of human limitations; more than one, struck with wonder, have declared that a character such as this could never have been invented by human ingenuity, that it walks through the four Gospels with the manifest consistency of truth, that the character of Jesus Christ alone commands the homage of mankind.

Let us watch Him and draw our own conclusions. First, with whom does He associate? For a man's favorite companions are often a sufficient indication of the man himself. With whom does He not? He is at home alike in the city and with the simple country people; He is welcomed alike at the tables of the rich and great, and in the cottages of the poor; scholars come to argue with Him, the ignorant and unskilled find in Him an understanding mind; He is the companion of those who aspire to high thoughts and noble deeds, and yet is taunted for being the associate of publicans and sinners; men and women are equally among His friends; He is at home in the public square, or discussing with a timid disciple in the silence of the night; He will magnetize an audience by the roadside with His words, friends and enemies, learned and unlearned, and even as He speaks the tiny children gather at His feet, and clamber on His knee, and cling about His neck, knowing very well that for all His greatness He is still theirs and of themselves.

Nor is this an affectation or a studied pose; it is not the fruit of careful training; there is throughout that ring of genuineness which makes all feel that indeed His soul understands, and His heart feels and sympathizes, and the love that He shows rings deep and true. Contradictory as it may seem to some, He is at once the friend of all and the friend of each; the more He is known, the more individuals cling about Him; Peter and John, Mary and Martha, the rich young man and the woman at the well, all find in Him complete and perfect union. And as He gave to others, so are others compelled to

give in return; for great as He is, there remains
that sense of equality about Him; though He
teaches with authority, though He works wonders, though He denounces the corrupt in high
places, though He claims for Himself that which
none ever dared to claim, withal He remains
"only Jesus," and in His company men find the
security of mutual surrender.

Or listen to His words and from them learn
the nature of the Man. He speaks by the roadside to the ignorant passers-by, things that they
understand, in language that comes from their
own lips, colored with the details of their own
lives; and yet while He speaks the learned in the
law and the Scripture gather round the group
and are baffled by the wisdom of His teaching,
and the grandeur of His words, and the truth
of His illustration that to this day ranks with
the highest eloquence, the sublimest poetry. At
once He is simple and great; familiar and of
the strictest dignity; strong with the strength
of a reformer, yet with the tears of weakness
trickling through His words; speaking as one
having authority, and yet with a note of appeal,
and pity, and almost of despair, ringing through
every address; succouring the downtrodden, for
they know that He knows, giving nerve to the
courageous, for they feel that He is with them,
drawing the hesitating, for they see that He has

discovered them, captivating and giving new life to the broken, and disillusioned, for He seems to have gone through the same, even His enemies at times being compelled to shake off the fascination, lest they too should be tied by the bond of His all-embracing sympathy, the rapture of His transparent truth.

"Never did man speak as this man hath spoken." The cry is freely echoed through all time; literature can find no parallel to the simple truth of His descriptions, the uniqueness of His parables, the vehemence of His denunciations, the pathos of His complaints, the point of His critical analysis, the exactness of His teaching; almost a strange thing is this, that one claims for Jesus Christ the first place in the use of human language, so small does such a claim appear in the halo of the Man Himself. For language, great as it is, is nevertheless a poor thing when it tries to express the full heart of a real man; there is much more in him than words can tell, there is much that can only be told by silence. Here He stood, pressed about by men, "so that he could not so much as eat bread," and His disciples said: "He is become mad"; and yet His delight was in the sweets of contemplation, alone in the silence of the night, on the quiet mountain side, away from men communing with God His Father. Those who knew

Him as they found Him, called Him the Master, the Teacher, and thronged about Him, asking for the Bread of Life; those who lived with Him, and knew Him best, would creep up the hillside in the early morning, and find Him lost in prayer, and would draw Him back among themselves with their simple petition: "Lord, teach us to pray."

Oh! this baffling Jesus Christ! We look for His striking characteristic, and we find He has none; His preferences, and there is none which stands out more than another. It is not that, stoic-like, He has subdued all His human longings; He possesses them all, keen and sensitive and vigorous, so that nothing that is capable of loves escapes the width of His all-embracing heart. The weeping widow cannot be passed by, the wailing cripple by the roadside must be heard; the penitent sinner must be made a bosom-friend, if so she can be raised to a new life and a brighter outlook; even the traitor shall not be betrayed, but shall be called "Friend!" to the last. Independent of them all He may be, strong to rebuke, bold to encourage, brave to face every criticism; yet the cry is in the heart, and sometimes breaks out in words, when the least of His friends is ungrateful, while for a word of recognition, a single confession of belief in Him, His thankful acknowledgment pours itself out in words and deeds that prove the depth of His human nature.

It is a hopeless task to compress into a single study all that may be said of this perfect Jesus Christ. We can only lay down the pen in despair, and say with St. John, that beloved and loving disciple: "There are also many other things that Jesus did: which if they were written, everyone, the world itself, I think, would not be able to contain the books that should be written." Sinless, so utterly unspotted, that not the most carping critic, no, not the most falsifying witness, could find in Him a word or a deed, that could be made a shadow of a charge; "Which of you shall accuse me of sin?" He could ask all the world, and the world had to confess that He was true to the marrow of His bones. Selfless; for who could think of Jesus Christ as self-seeking, this Jesus Christ who could be taunted on His cross as One "who saved others, but himself could not save." In the world, yet not in the world; of the world, yet not of the world; the Lord of men, yet their servant; their greatest, yet the meekest and humblest; "beautiful among the sons of men," yet "there was no beauty in him"; adored of men, yet "despised and rejected"; lover of men, loved of men, yet men cried that He should be crucified; where shall the litany stop? We draw it all into one; the

63

portrait is complete; too tremendous not to be stamped deep in the least sympathetic. St. Paul looks at it and is overwhelmed. Here, he says, is perfect humanity; its solution is in this only, that it is also divine; and at the end of his days he can only sum up his final message to his own in this: "Put ye on the Lord Jesus Christ." That is to be the perfect man.

THE PASSION OF CHRIST

WHEN the four evangelists come to speak of the
Passion and Death of Jesus Christ a marked
change comes over them all. Hitherto they had
picked and chosen, as events suited their pur-
poses; much they had omitted, about the order
they were not exact, the life of Jesus Christ, in
the modern understanding of the term, none of
them had attempted to describe. But with the
scenes of the Passion all is different; now step
by step they follow the Master, from His Last
Supper on Thursday night to His lying in the
tomb on Friday evening; it is clear that they
all wish to emphasize the accurate historic truth
of that which they are so careful to narrate.

One may well ask why they are so anxious to
bring out the fact of the Passion more than of
anything else in His life. They made so much
of the Lord, they had looked forward with such
eagerness to the kingdom and their place in it,
even afterwards His glory was so paramount in
their minds, that one might well suppose they
would not have been too ready to dwell upon the

day of His humiliation. But perhaps this is the very reason for their opposite choice. For the Passion was a revelation to them; it was the great correction of all their false ideas. By it and in it they understood at last the significance of many prophecies, of which hitherto they had been able to make nothing, and which they had quietly ignored. In it they learned the true nature of the King and Kingdom, which the most explicit words had been unable to teach. The Passion, when later they put the whole revelation of Jesus Christ together, was to them more than an episode in His life; it was the crowning of all, the light in which all else was to be interpreted, both that which was past and that which was yet to be. "O foolish, and slow of heart to believe in all things which the prophets have spoken. Ought not Christ to have suffered these things, and so to enter into his glory? And beginning at Moses and all the prophets, he expounded to them in all the scriptures the things that were concerning him." It was when they had understood this that they made so much of the Passion.

Nor need we do more here than dwell on the historic fact; the meaning of the Passion can only come by meditation, and it will come in proportion to our acceptance of Jesus Christ Himself. If He is to us no more than a mere man, then the Passion is no more than another human tragedy among many; an act of injustice, a gross violation of the law, but hardly enough to make the Cross an emblem of triumph or of charity. If to us He is more than man, if He is that for which He Himself said that He lived and died, then is the Cross consecrated; the acknowledgment of the one is the acknowledgment of the other.

The end had come, swiftly and unexpectedly. Before, His enemies had fixed on times and places when they would apprehend Him, but invariably they had failed; now they decided among themselves that the time and place were opportune, but it was "their hour and the power of darkness," and a strange infatuation led them on. Before, He had been warned and had defied all warning; now He prepared Himself with the deliberation of one who knew. A day of retirement, a last meal in which He bade a loving farewell to His own, an agony of loneliness on a hillside when the blood oozed out of every pore, the acceptance of a kiss from a traitor, whom nevertheless, He would not injure or betray, and He was ready to receive His executioners, and let them do with Him what they would.

They held Him and bound His hands behind His back; then down the hill, and across the brook, and along the rocky path on the other side, until they reached the city. In at the gate and to the house of the old man, Annas, the crafty controller of the high-priesthood. There were judges waiting for Him; they had their will at last; and while prudence advised some show of trial, hatred betrayed them into shame. He was struck in the face; He was spat upon by these high lords as they passed out; that was the end of His first trial.

From Annas to Caiphas, the actual high priest. Here, more show of form, more connivance of the court; but the issue is very little different. From the court to prison; left all night to the mercy of a brutal soldiery, by nature cruel, by training hardened to all pity, by service knowing well that maltreatment of this Victim will not be displeasing to their masters.

Early morning, and the drama must be hurried on: it must at all costs be concluded before sunset, or these holy men will be defiled. So once more a hurried trial, with mock dignity, to confirm the decision of the night before; and then a hustling, shrieking procession through the city, that the august representative of Rome may do their will for them. But the representative of Rome is not inclined to act; their vehemence betrays their motive, their cause is ill-defined and shifting, there must be something in this broken man more than can be seen, to rouse such hatred against Him; he had better

leave the case alone. Is He a Galilæan? Then
to Herod the Galilæan He shall be referred; that
man, at all events, with blood already on his
hands, and a heart that luxury has sapped of all
feeling, will find it easy to do this people's will.

But Herod is too cunning; he will not so easily
be trapped into usurpation of the Roman power;
he will be content with the cruelty of fooling.
And so Jesus Christ is dragged along to him,
is befooled by him before the court of His own
Galilæans, and is again dragged back to Pilate
the Roman for His final sentence. Still Pilate
will not act; perhaps with a little this blood-
thirsty mob will be satisfied; he will have Him
degraded beyond recognition; he will chastise
Him, and then, perhaps, will be able to let Him
go.

So a second time Jesus Christ is given to men
trained in brutality; this time not permitted, but
ordered to do their worst. He is dragged down
the steps into the courtyard; His clothes are
torn from Him, and He stands naked before this
ribald crew; His hands are tied to a low pillar,
His back is bent: there is no defense for the
tender bones against the heavy lashes that now
fall on Him thick and fast. The blood soon flows in
streams; the flesh-wounds gape open; at last the
writhing body slips in its own blood, and, while
the hands are still tied above, crouches like a

hiding hare about the pillar. Still the blows fall, now upon the tender upturned face and breast; till the cord is cut, and the quivering thing rolls helplessly upon the ground.

But this is not enough; there is sport in this creature, and the game shall be carried on. He said He was a King; then a King He shall be made. An old box shall serve as His throne, a soldier's scarlet mantle shall be His royal robe, a reed shall make His sceptre, for His crown there is nothing better than the prickly brushwood that serves as fuel for the fire. A soldier hacks a piece of this away; with his sword and his baton he beats it into a ball; he plumps it upon the head of the Victim and hammers it there till it is helmet-shaped; the head rolls in agony; the helmet-crown is in danger of falling; a cord of reed-leaves will serve the purpose; it is twisted round the thorns, fixed, knotted, and behold the King of the Jews is crowned!

There follows the oath of mock allegiance, that the show might be completed. "Hail, King!" "Prophesy unto us!" And in many other ways did they insult Him. Then suddenly the play is ended. A message from the Governor; the criminal must be sent to him at once. "Unfit to be seen?" So much the better; perhaps at the sight of Him the mob will be appeased. So He is again dragged forward, still wearing the soldier's mantle, with the thorny helmet still upon His head, bent double beneath the torture of His wounds, His hands behind His back, His eyes blood-clotted, His mouth not daring to close itself for thirst, His tongue hanging loose upon the lower lip, not a sound part to be seen upon His body, "a worm and no man"; is it wonderful that Pilate introduced Him with the words: "Look at the man!"

But the device availed nothing, as half yielding to a tempter never does avail. He must be crucified; that only will suffice. So the sentence is passed. He is dressed again in His own clothes; two planks for His cross are put upon His shoulder, two others are set with Him, to be His companions in death; guards go before, one holding aloft the statement of His crime: "Jesus of Nazareth, the King of the Jews." Through the streets the procession passes; out at the gate, for the city must not be polluted by an execution within its walls. His clothes are torn from Him; He is thrown upon the ground; His arms are stretched along one plank to their farthest limit, secured with cords, and then nails are driven through the hands. The other plank is fixed into the ground; the Victim is raised and the plank to which He is fastened is nailed across the other: cord is put about His waist;

His feet are raised and nailed flat against the lower plank; and Jesus Christ is crucified.

Three hours more of intolerable, writhing agony, while the people howl, while the Mother and a few faithful ones look on in horror, while the very sun hides itself in shame. One loud cry, and then the end. A soldier runs his spear through the side; the people shrink away in remorse, now that the deed is done; a centurion cries: "Indeed this was the Son of God!" and the body of Jesus Christ hangs between heaven and earth, appealing to men, appealing to God, appealing from that day till the end of time.

THE RESURRECTION

THAT Our Lord Jesus Christ actually and really died upon the Cross on Calvary there can be no reasonable doubt. The facts of the case are so clearly given, the evidence is so detailed and circumstantial, that it is only foolish, romantic, and unscientific minds that would venture to bring it into question. For instance, a novelist such as Marie Corelli, in her bitter reaction against Christianity, is able with her diseased imagination to distort the facts, makes of Judas a much-abused man, a saint of Barabbas, of Peter a despicable creature, and then goes on to describe Jesus Christ recovering from coma in the tomb; but for all this she has not a trace of evidence, nor does she pretend to have any but that of a feeble woman's fancy.

On the side of historic fact, in contrast with sentiment, the proofs are overwhelmingly convincing. The sufferings of the Passion are alone sufficient to bring death to an ordinary man, even if the crucifixion itself were omitted. The soldiers were given orders to see that the criminals were dead by a certain hour; before that hour they had convinced themselves that Jesus was dead; to have made a mistake under circumstances such as these was impossible. To prove the fact, one of them ran his spear through the body; there came forth blood and water; medical authority will tell you that this certainly means death. The corpse was taken down; it passed through the hands of enemies and friends; the former gave it freely to the latter; had there been a shadow of doubt about the death this could never have happened.

Another fact is evident; not only to His friends was Jesus Christ quite dead, but with Him had died all their hopes and expectations. They ceased to look for a new kingdom; they slunk away into hiding; they began to wonder at the meaning of so many promises upon which their hopes had been founded: it was only a lingering love which still held them up, for with all their disappointments they still felt the truth, and worth, and fascination of Him whom they had lost. On the other hand His enemies had grown arrogant. They now showed that after all they had understood Jesus Christ far better than they had pretended, far better, in some respects, than the disciples themselves; had there been a doubt about His death they would never have so given themselves away. While He lived they had affected to misunderstand His words: "Destroy this temple, and in three days I will build it up again"; now when indeed the temple had been destroyed, they were quick to make sure, so far as they could make sure, that destroyed it should remain.

Then suddenly we have a transformation, one which is accomplished in exactly fifty days. These timid followers of Jesus Christ, who had seen Him die, whose hopes had been annihilated, who had gone back to their fishing and ordinary lives, suddenly, one and all, without a single exception, backed up by many more behind them, come out into the world, the world of their enemies, before whom they had slunk cowed and turned craven, and proclaim that this Jesus Christ is not dead but living, that they had all seen Him with their own eyes, that He had been dead—yes—but that He had risen again, and that after all the Kingdom had begun. They went forth and proclaimed this fact, contradictory as it was to all human experience, in itself at first so absurd; they proclaimed it to men whose instincts, and prejudices, and experience, and reason, and common sense, were against it, and who had the means at hand of refuting the statement if they chose; yet of these they converted many thousands in a single morning. This fact was always the uppermost in their teaching;

upon it they built all the rest; its acceptance was made the test for all who proposed to be their followers; for it they lived, in the certainty of it they died; there is no other fact of history which has evidence such as this, none so vividly attested.

To put it in its mildest form, this phenomenon demands explanation. The very least human materialist cannot study the suddenness of this transformation in the "witnesses of the Resurrection," without asking himself what was its cause; he cannot see this witness carried on through all time to our own, increasing in volume without ceasing, accepted by men of common sense and judgment in every generation, but he must ask himself what is the basis upon which all this rests. He goes to the evidences, and he is compelled to acknowledge they are sound; so sound that a man who would ignore them in any other case would be deemed an unfit historian. The knowledge of Alexander the Great and of his empire is based on far less evidence; the power of Julius Cæsar is not more authentically proved; in a court of law, were it but a question of the matter of fact, the evidence would be overwhelming.

No; it is not the historic evidence that is wanting for the fact of the Resurrection; it is not the unreliability of the witnesses, who were themselves convinced almost against their will and judgment, who were tested sufficiently at the time, and who laid down their lives for the truth of what they taught; it is the matter of fact itself that is the obstacle. Let a man make up his mind, definitely and certainly, that a thing cannot be, and no evidence in the world will convince him; but then it may be that it is not the evidence but himself that is at fault. The thing may not after all be unreasonable, but it may be himself who refuses to listen to reason. Let a man decide within himself, before he begins his investigation, that the Resurrection of Jesus Christ could never have taken place, and therefore did never take place, and he will not have much difficulty with the rest. He can easily then persuade himself, first, that the witnesses must have been dishonest or deluded, because they affirm something which he has made up his mind shall not be true; and second, that the evidence must be faulty, because as it stands it convicts him of error. But this is not to listen to reason; it is judgment formed on other grounds than reason, whatever those grounds may be.

To listen to reason is to recognize first of all reason's estimate of itself. Man, says reason, is a very finite creature; there are many things he can do, but many more things he cannot; many truths he can understand, but many more he cannot. And his reason is like himself, finite and feeble; it can reach a certain distance, it can guess at distances which it cannot reach, but the farther it reaches, and the more it guesses— that is, the better it is educated—so much the more does it realize the infinite spaces of knowledge which are utterly beyond its grasp.

Reason, therefore, when it comes across a truth, or a supposed truth, which of itself it cannot grasp, is only reasonable when it tries some other test, not when it trusts merely to itself. Trusting to itself it is bound to fail; for then on its own confession it is attempting the impossible. To say a thing is not true, merely because I cannot understand it, is very much like the fox who said the grapes were sour, merely because he could not jump high enough to reach them.

So it is with the fact of the Resurrection. That the dead should rise again, the fact of it, the manner of it, is beyond all human understanding. Aristotle even maintains that the fact of life after death is beyond the power of man on earth to grasp; but not on that account does he deny it. Since, then, we know nothing at all about it, our only means of learning must be sought elsewhere; all that reason can do is to sift the evidence, and see whether it is sufficient;

if it denies beforehand the conclusion, it is acting beyond its powers.

What, then, is the evidence? There came a man on earth who by word and deed won for Himself a claim to utter truthfulness. This man declared that He had come from God, that He was the Messenger of God, that He was the Son of God. He was asked for a final proof of His message and He gave it; not merely the miracles that He wrought, not merely the sublimity of His own personal character, not only the wonder of His teaching; but He would give them a proof that would stagger humanity itself, that could witness to superhuman power and nothing less, the power not only of life and death, but of the life and death of Himself. At an appointed time His enemies should be permitted to destroy Him; three days after He would walk again upon the earth.

Such is the astonishing statement of this otherwise utterly truthful Man. Coming from another mouth, no matter how truthful, the declaration could have excited only two feelings: ridicule or pity. But His words aroused neither. His enemies heard them, and understood them, and feared them after He was dead; His friends heard them, and understood them not, only after He had risen again did they realize them. For He promised, and He kept His promise; He kept

His promise, and proved it by evidence sufficient
to establish any fact in history; He pointed to
the past as foreshadowing this event; He pointed
to the future as its outcome; let man ask for
any test whatsoever, short of that of actually
himself being present, and he will find that it is
satisfied in the evidence of the Resurrection—
for the man, that is, of goodwill.

How like God is this! Like Him in His condescension, like Him in His mightiness, like Him,
too, in that wonderful subtlety by which He
leaves man free to choose or not. The evidence
is there, but man is not compelled to take it.
To the lover of Christ it is abundantly sufficient;
His enemy need not believe. "Blessed are they
who have not seen and have believed."

THE JUDGMENT OF ANNAS

"The high priest then asked Jesus of his disciples and his doctrine."—John xviii. 19.

IT is one of the characteristics of the dealings of God with man that from beginning to end the will and choice of man should be free. No matter how vital the consequences of the choice, whether to the man in himself, or even to the whole human race, still man shall not be forced to choose what is true, to do what is right, except by the choice that comes from his own heart. No matter how deep, how important, how inspiring the truth which He has revealed, still there is always around it just sufficient mist and cloud to allow the man of bad will, the man who wishes not to see, to find reason enough to follow his own bent.

In other words, by a marvelous act of condescension, God and His Christ have submitted themselves to the tribunal of mankind in the economy of this world; the choice of faith is what we mean by man's acceptance of God in this tribunal of his own individual conscience. Each man is judge in his own court; Jesus Christ comes before him, with His credentials in His hand and the witnesses for and against Him; the question at issue is far too vital and tremendous to be dismissed with an evasive "not proven"; "He that is not with him is against him"; every man who has once come to know Him either accepts Him or does not; and the result of the sentence is either the dominion of Jesus Christ in that particular heart or His dismissal, with consequences tremendous for all time and for all eternity.

But man is not a simple creature; he is the resultant of many forces; forces from the distant past, and still more from those of his own accepting. His eye does not see with that precision which reason usually demands; his mind and thought are influenced by the weight of his own preconceptions; when he comes to choose, especially in matters concerning his own life, the meaning of right and wrong, the significance of Jesus Christ, habit enslaves his will, self-interest bends his judgment, passion blinds and hurries his reason, and he decides, too often, the question whether He is or is not by the mere consideration of what he wishes Him to be. If Jesus Christ mattered nothing to man, no doubt the whole world would acknowledge Him; but He matters so much, the acceptance of Him implies so many consequences, that men turn on their heels and mutter: "This is a hard saying and who shall hear it," and "from that day walk with him no more."

In the divine economy Jesus Christ during His own lifetime was set before many judges. He was tried and condemned not once but many times; and each time there was displayed some feature of our human nature which from His day till now has played its part in the blinding of men. It is a study well worth our while to consider these judges; the understanding of them may teach us something of the way men look at Him today; it may teach us something of our own selves.

First, He was brought before Annas. What a strange beginning is this! The late high-priest, with no claim now to the title, yet so associated with it, and so powerful in the appointment to the office, that men easily gave him the name, and whatever material dignity belonged to it. A man whom all feared and none loved; whose religion was frankly the wielding of power among his people; the type of power and success; the hand behind the machine of politics, whether

Jewish or Roman, with wealth untold to confirm his views; with no conscience-scruples to hinder his action, no thought of life after death or follies of that nature; he lived for this world, and for all this world could give him, and religion was as useful for his purpose as any other tool. As for this Jesus Christ, this so-called Messias, to such a man He was merely a nuisance; He disturbed the routine of life, He stirred up trouble that was much better ignored; justice or no justice the Man must be got out of the way.

Before this man stood Jesus Christ on His first trial. Of Himself Annas asked nothing; what were or were not His claims were of no account to him; more important was it to know who were His associates, how far His influence extended, what precisely was the teaching on which this influence was founded. Hence the summary sentence of the Evangelist: "The high-priest then asked Jesus of his disciples and his doctrine"; it is the questioning of one who has no intention to learn; of one who is satisfied with his own authority, and will have none of this arrogant intruder.

To him as to all the world is the same answer made. Jesus Christ is no crafty dealer; there is no underhand method about Him; He is the founder of no secret society; if he wished to know the truth let him ask those who had heard

Him. And as for the inquiry concerning His disciples He would say nothing. Their turn would some day come; for "the servant was not greater than his master," and if the self-satisfied power of this world persecuted Him, they, too, in their turn would one day be persecuted. But for the present they should be shielded. There was no apologetic yielding in the reply; there was the dignity of truth, the superiority of innocence, the boldness almost of defiance and appeal in His words, which have often enough since been repeated before the tribunal of men: "I have spoken openly to the world; I have always taught in the Synagogue and in the Temple, whither all the Jews resort; and in private I have spoken nothing. Why askest thou me? Ask them who have heard what I have spoken to them; behold they know what things I have said."

But justice — how often! — is a conditional thing; and never more than when Jesus Christ, "his disciples and his doctrines," are on their trial. For "justice" assumes its omnipotence; the powers that be will not brook contradiction, especialy such power as is frankly in the world and of the world; did not Jesus Christ Himself teach his followers: "Upon the chair of Moses have sitten the Scribes and Pharisees. Whatsoever they shall bid you observe and do"? Therefore such arrogance as this cannot be tolerated.

This Jesus Christ, whoever He may be, shall be condemned, if only for contempt of court; and the cold eye of scorn looks out upon Him, and the evidence of truth is ignored, and in the name of justice justice is set aside, by one whose authority was legally nothing.

Justice such as this has an abundance of supporters. There will always be those standing by to whom might is the same thing as right, who will support the hand that has the gold, and the dignity, and the seat of office, and to whom justice is the same thing as obeisance. Let such an authority show that he is offended, and vengeance shall be wreaked on the offender, be he who he may; how many times, in the name of worldly dignity offended, has defenseless innocence been struck down, whose only crime was this, that it pleaded its innocence before a court that had willed it to be guilty? What but this is the explanation of the bloody persecutions of truth that have stained the history of man? Right then was it that He who was all truth should set this example to His own: "And when he had said these things, one of the officers standing by gave Jesus a blow, saying, "Answerest thou the high-priest so?"

But truth is not silenced by a blow. Though it may not be heard, nay, though indignity is piled upon indignity because of its insistence, though in the end death alone is the penalty, still truth will appeal; not for compensation, not for its rights, but for the simple justice that is due of the meanest. Hence, with His face tingling from the blow, with the livid lines already rising and disfiguring His features, while worldly "justice" looks on and is silent, saying to itself, "What is this to us?" ignoring its own responsibility, and the provocation it has given, Truth Itself turns to Its assailant and appeals, in terms similar to those It has used before. To the materialist judge, whose horizon was limited to the world around him, Jesus Christ had offered the evidence of that very world; for the sycophant soldier, the limit of whose motive was an affected indignation, He had but a sobering answer: "If I have spoken ill, give testimony of the evil, but if well, why strikest thou me?"

So ends this trial before materialism. In all this world there is no power that can act with such pretense of justice, even with such a show of condescending charity, as can the materialist, the self-appointed judge of all truth. Accept his final word, and all is well; be of no significance in his eyes, and he will treat you with consideration. But let it once appear that truth is against him and on your side, that your doctrine denies his assumptions, that there are disciples who listen to this teaching, and the sentence is already passed, be evidence what it may; and when nothing else is to be said, the upholder of truth is insulted, and disfigured truth is handed on to another judge, and Annas passes out of his court well satisfied that this intruder is no longer to be feared.

The case against the world is plain; but in the heart of every man how much of this spirit lies hidden; Truth stands in judgment before all and each, and so long as it matters nothing she is easily accepted. But let it once be seen that she will interfere, that our own material satisfaction is at stake, then perhaps we hear more easily the sound of the blow upon her face; when she is struck, and we can point to her as degraded, it is less difficult to pass her by.

THE JUDGMENT OF CAIPHAS

"It is expedient that one man should die for the people."—John xi. 50.

THE worldling passes by Jesus Christ; he has nothing in common with Him; if He is struck it matters little, let Him look to His own protection. But there is another high-priest of this world who finds it not so easy to dismiss Jesus Christ and His claims, and his followers are far more numerous. For among those who have once been touched by the sense of truth and of God, the downright worldling is not commonly found; and when he is found he betrays himself by signs that cannot be mistaken. More common —indeed is he not wellnigh universal?—is the man who has felt the attraction, and yet feels no less the drawing on the other side; who would have Jesus Christ, and yet would not lose his hold upon this world; who would serve at once God and Mammon; and who in the end, since he has attempted the impossible, finds reason enough to set Jesus Christ aside.

In truth man is a wonderful self-deceiver. As a child he has little to trouble him; but scarcely has the business of life begun than he learns to weigh consequences. He still goes along his way, the votary of truth, the upholder of right conduct; to hear him speak one might say that he is the same as ever, nay, that he is now more sincere than in the days of his first simplicity. But in matter of fact many things have happened. He has met other minds which have deeply affected his own; he has become associated with other companions, who seem to have a stronger hold on life; he has met with fresh experiences, which have made him reflect on his first principles and ask himself whether they are right; last of all, his eyes have looked into the future, his heart has gone out in some ambition, his hand has itched to grasp some special object, and he has pondered whether to all this his present hold on truth is not a hindrance.

At once he is tempted to make some kind of compromise. He would not let go the truth which he possesses; indeed he feels and knows the truth will not let him go. At the same time, he tells himself, he must live in harmony with all that is about him. He must be free in mind as are others; he must be as daring and independent in his manner of life; he must learn from experience, and gain yet more; he must strive to attain his ambitions. What can there be wrong in all this, And if truth as he knows it tells him there is danger, then perhaps truth itself misunderstands, or is misunderstood. Perhaps truth has not grasped the whole situation. Perhaps there are reasons on the other side. Perhaps things are not so wrong as instinct and training dictate. Perhaps some can be found who will show him that truth itself is not wholly true. Perhaps—

And by degrees the struggling creature succeeds in defending the service of its two masters. It will serve truth, but just so far and no farther; to serve it farther is not wise, is not convenient, is not expedient. But truth urges; for truth cannot be silenced. Then, once the initial step has been made, the rest is easy. Perhaps truth is not wholly true; there are many reasons why it may not be true; I wish and hope it may be found not to be true; I am determined it shall not be true; it is not true; I will be right, and truth shall be put in the wrong. But if truth is in the wrong, then truth is a usurper, and therefore must be punished. And so, by subtle argument, with all the time a show of uprightness, and justice, and virtue, truth is first questioned, then ignored, then condemned, and last of all is submitted to every indignity, to the worst kinds of human cruelty.

Jesus Christ stood before Caiphas and the assembled chief priests. Already He had been found inconvenient for their way of life; long before, therefore, the sentence had been passed, with every show of pompous righteousness: "It is expedient that one man should die for the people." "It is expedient!" Therefore, at whatever cost, His conviction must be secured. The show of righteousness shall be preserved; we must be seen the upholders of truth, the seekers after truth, even while we pass sentence; let witness then be found, true or false it matters little, provided only it be specious, that this Jesus Christ may be put out of the way.

But it is the way of falsehood to be inconsistent; false witnesses cannot agree; it is only when men have decided beforehand that they shall agree that they gain a hearing. "And the chief-priests and all the council sought false witness against Jesus, that they might put him to death, and they found none. For many bore false witness against him, and their evidence did not agree." No, not even though they pretended to quote His very words against Him: "We have heard him say, I am able to destroy this temple of God, made with hands; and in three days I will build another not made with hands." The judges knew too well the travesty contained in this evidence; the very next day they showed that they had understood the truth when they demanded; "Sir, we have remembered, that that seducer said, while he was yet alive, After three days I will rise again. Command, therefore, the sepulchre to be guarded until the third day, lest his disciples come, and steal him away, and say to the people, He is risen from the dead; so that the last error shall be worse than the first."

But knowledge of the truth matters little when "it is expedient" that truth shall die. The witnesses had failed; but they were not discarded for their falsehood. The last evidence was manifestly garbled; yet not on that account must truth prevail. In spite of all the contradictions it must be assumed that there is fact somewhere underlying this mass of evidence; how easily can men so escape self-condemnation ! So does Caiphas escape; so out of falsehood is he able still to support his case. "And the high-priest, rising up in the midst, asked Jesus, saying, Answerest thou nothing to the things that are laid to thy charge by these men?"

What splendid affectation ! It is no concern of mine, he seems to say; he who had declared it expedient that this man should die. It is merely a question of justice, he implies; he who had already determined which way the sentence should go. If the witnesses one by one are merely despicable, yet the sum total must mean something; this alone betrays the will that is shaping the final judgment. In the whole of human history have any more enemies of truth been found than the many imitators of Caiphas?

But truth has its own reply, and to falsehood its best reply is silence. Jesus "held his peace, and answered nothing." Then, since falsehood could not prevail, since accumulated evidence was futile, out of His own mouth He should be convicted. He should be compelled to tell the truth; but in such a way, and in such an assembly, that the very truth itself should be evidence sufficient. It was a risk, and the high-priest knew it; for truth might be taken at its word, and then this Christ would be triumphant. But the risk must be run; after all he had influence, and hatred, and his own consummate acting on his side. "Again the high-priest asked him, and said to him, I adjure thee by the living God, that thou tell us, if thou be the Christ the Son of the blessed God. And Jesus said to him, I am. Nevertheless I say to you, Hereafter you shall see the Son of Man sitting on the right hand of the power of God and coming in the clouds of heaven."

In the history of man was ever question more momentous put than this? Let us consider it well. Caiphas was the high-priest of Jewry. If any man knew, he knew the meaning of his words. He wished and intended, in this last resort, to convict Christ Jesus of blasphemy out of His own mouth. But that blasphemy might be even charged, these words must be taken literally. The words: "Christ, the Son of the blessed God" must mean exactly what they say; the claimant to the title must claim to be God; anything less would involve no blasphemy. Caiphas knew it; Jesus Christ knew it, too; here, then, when He said in open court: "I am," He was asked to state whether He was God; for the first time His answer was explicit; He was explicitly so understood by those who heard Him; and they were left to choose whether they would take Him, or whether they would reject Him, without any doubt whatsoever in their minds.

It was a dreadful moment; one the like of which millions of men will do anything to evade. They will accept Jesus Christ as great Master; or they will pass Him by as no concern of theirs; they will admire others who choose Him outright; but for themselves they will not face the dilemma. And here the court for a moment hesitated; the shock was too much, the emphatic words of the Victim were tremendous; the responsibility in the choice was infinite in its effects. Not a moment was to be lost. Before the hearers decided they must be swayed, and the high-priest knew how "inexpedient" it would be were Christ to be dismissed. "Then the high-priest rent his garments, saying, He hath blasphemed. What further need have we of witnesses? Behold, now you have heard the blasphemy. What think you? But they all answering said, He is guilty of death."

The ruse succeeded; how often since has a single word turned the scale among hesitating men, even in our own hesitating hearts! And when the scale has been turned, then woe betide the upholder of truth; no disgrace is too disgraceful.

"And some began to spit on him, and to buffet him. And the men that held him smote him on the face, mocked him, and struck him. And they blindfolded him, and struck his face with the palms of their hands and they asked him, saying, Prophesy unto us, O Christ, who is it that struck thee? And many other things, blaspheming, they said against him."

THE JUDGMENT OF HEROD

"The soul of the wicked desireth evil; he will not have pity on his neighbor."—*Prov. xxi. 10.*

JESUS CHRIST Our Lord lived by far the greater part of His life in the hill country of Galilee, and all the time He lived there He had for the ruler of His land a man in many ways remarkable. To what nationality he belonged it was hard to say; he could call himself a Jew or a Gentile as he pleased, and in his life he partook of the nature of both. He was a son of that Herod who had massacred the Innocents at Bethlehem, he had inherited his father's evil nature, with little of his overwhelming strength; only at times would a certain reckless daring flicker up, and impel him to acts of shameless cruelty, only to be followed with reactions of weakness, and fear, and superstition, and despair. Being neither Greek nor Jew, his manner of life was Greek or Jewish as he pleased; in his favorite city of Tiberias he gathered round himself the luxury and grandeur of the West, in Magdala close by the riches and luxury of the East were gathered together for his enjoyment.

It is not hard to imagine for ourselves the manner of life that this man led. Love was not in it; such a man is never loved. Instead, were all the substitutes of love; the sycophant attendants on wealth and luxury, the flattering of courtiers who spat behind his back, the revelry, the eating and drinking and dancing and confusion, that such a man will welcome, whether to silence conscience, or to make himself imagine he is happy, or to keep around him the band of followers who are bound to him by no other tie. A restless, empty, pleasure-seeking round, every cup tasted, every satisfaction played out, looking always for something new and strange to relieve the weary monotony, loud in its laughter, loud in its anger, night turned to day, and the day spent in darkness of body and of soul—such is the life that we read between the lines of the Scripture story.

Being what he was, it is not wonderful that Herod Antipas made little account of what men really thought of him. The beginner in evil may be influenced by shame; the poor debauched victim is shameless; and Herod had plunged too deep in indulgence either to endure any further restraint, or to care very much for the opinion of others. Hence he lives openly in adultery, and defies anyone to criticize; to suit the whim of a mere dancing girl he steeps his hands in human blood, defying by his deed even the people he governed, for John the Baptist was esteemed and loved among them. It is true all this was not done with impunity; fear and superstition made him see a haunting ghost ever on his track; but he kept a brave face upon it all, he grew in cruelty, and the murder of John did but make him the more ready for the hunting down of Jesus Christ Himself.

No; Herod is not hard to understand; we have too many like him about us, perhaps we have enough experience of him in our own poor hearts. Vice, and even tampering with vice, may have its fascination; it may give us something of the "knowledge of good and evil," as the father of all vices foretold; but it robs us of much more than it gives, it disgusts much more than it fascinates; if it brings its pleasure and life for a moment, it brings as well endless misery and death. Vice makes us untrue, in thought, in word, and in action; vice makes us weak, helpless slaves at the mercy of our most hated tormentors; vice, like some foul internal leprosy, eats up the beauty that was ours, of soul and of body; vice leaves us hardened, and loveless, and incapable of loving, suspicious, and merciless, even to wanton brutality. If vice were not in the world there would be no need for an hereafter; only when it came did God need to bring death with it; for to leave men here, once it had found a home among them, would have been to condemn them to a living hell.

When, then, Herod, the man built up of such material, had at last Jesus Christ Our Lord in his clutches, it is easy to follow and interpret his treatment of Him. Much as he had feared Him when He was free, and sought to take His life, now when he held Him a prisoner bound he was glad, and thought to have sport and amusement with Him. Luxury and vice do not usually begin with violence; they are soothing and cajoling at first. And so this Herod, judging others by himself, giving the living Truth and Sanctity credit for being no better than himself, begins with gentle words, pities His misfortunes, offers Him His freedom for a price; let Him but humor the onlookers, let Him but do a miracle for their amusement, and all would be well.

But truth is not easily cajoled; Innocence sincere is proof against flattery or bribe; yielding a little, even to gain much, is not the way of perfect Sanctity. And so Jesus stands there ignoring His tempter; between them there is nothing in common; not even His pitiful condition can bring Him to listen to the terms. Then vice, as is the way with vice, swings round to the other extreme. If Truth cannot be won by gentle words, if Innocence cannot be seduced by flattery, it shall be forced by harder means; it shall be told that it stands there on trial for its life, that if it does not yield it shall be shamed before all the world, that one word can save it, one act can make its life secure. But woe betide it if it is obstinate; if it is too proud to do as other people, then it shall be left to its doom.

Still Truth is silent; it will not cast its pearls before swine; the way of self-indulgence, the path of vice, does not lead to truth, whether human or divine. No man is more positive in his own defense than the man who is the victim of himself; and that is because he knows so little, cannot see farther than himself, is blind to the greater understanding which selflessness and innocence make clear. Truth is silent; truth is master of the field; and Herod, hitherto so confident, feels his very throne slipping from beneath him, feels again the ghost standing behind, looks around at his courtiers and knows too well that they execrate him, that they reverence the silent Monarch in their midst, even though they join with Herod for the time in

adding to His public degradation. Cajolery has
failed, threatening has failed; there is another
course which will always succeed when everything else comes to nothing. So Jesus Christ,
you are silent, are you? Then we will treat you
as a tongue-tied fool. You are "unco guid," you
are better than the rest of us, are you? Then
we will clothe you in the robe of baby-innocence,
and have you laughed at by the knowing world.
You defy our threats, do you? Then we will let
men see how we contemn you, we will not even
put you to death, but you shall go free, the
scum of men, not fit to stand in our company.
This last insult is the least pardonable of all;
you have almost turned the laughter against me;
Jesus Christ, innocent and truthful and holy—
we will have you laughed at for each of these,
now in my court and always.

And indeed Herod has succeeded. I have met
many a soul whose innocence and truth were
proof against every other trial; but before this
test they have wavered. Sin in itself they have
hated; it has never had any attraction for them.
Cajolery and flattery they have repudiated; these
have but stirred their indignation. Threats have
not affected them, except to strengthen them to
fight. But when men have laughed, and have
jeered at their innocence, and have mocked their
simplicity, and have made fun of their truth-

fulness, and have paraded before their eyes their own tawdry pomps and have pitied the drab garb of truth, then it has been hard to bear. They do not wish to sin, yet neither do they wish to be pointed at by others as peculiar. They have hated sin, yet they hate no less to be hated by their neighbors. Truth and innocence are treasures beyond price, yet perhaps they are the price to be paid that one may understand and enjoy the perhaps greater treasures of life.

"And Herod with his army set him at nought and mocked him, putting on him a white garment."—Thus did He endure the shame of being true, the disgrace of being sinless, the ridicule of being peculiar. And yet Jesus "knew what was in man," and, fool as man made Him, innocence looked straight through the hearts of them all. While they laughed at Him, He pitied them; while they saw in Him, or affected to see in Him, nothing but matter for amusement, He saw in them not only motive for forgiveness but also that deeper soul within which still kept His love for them alive. Let us not forget it. Herod and his court had set the tone to the gay life of Magdala. Once Jesus Himself had been at Magdala; He had sat with these men at table; even there they had watched Him, and carped, and criticized; yet He had carried away from that wicked place one single heart that the life of Magdala had ruined, and He pieced it again together, and out of it made a precious thing, and placed it inside His own. So different in effect are the manners of innocence and vice. Vice crushes the human heart and leaves it bleeding on the roadside; innocence picks it up, and cherishes it, and gives it of its own life.

THE JUDGMENT OF PILATE

"A perverse heart is abominable to the Lord: and his will is in them that walk sincerely."—Prov. xi. 20.

WHEN we read the lives of great apostles three things strike us as characteristic of them all. They are marked in the cries of the ancient prophets; in the life of Jesus Christ they may be said to be the dominant notes; in later teachers of truth they repeat themselves without any exception. They are, first, an intense realization and certainty of a particular truth which has sunk into them; second, an intense, all-mastering desire to impart this truth to others, that it may do for them what it has done for the teacher himself; and third, the cross of the apostle's life, the discovery, which grows with growing experience, that the chief obstacle to the spread of truth is not, as men so often say, its obscurity, not the confusion of the times, not the difficulty of circumstances, but the simple fact that man does not want it, and therefore will not have it, and in consequence by every means seeks to stifle its appeal.

It is easy to illustrate this truth. "Thou wouldst not," rings out in the words of Our Lord, and it is because they "would not," not so much because they were otherwise wicked, that the curse is pronounced on Corozain and Bethsaida, on Jerusalem, on the "Scribes and Pharisees, hypocrites," and lastly on His own chosen people. St Paul is not less pathetic; it is when he sees the men of Athens frivolously playing with the truth, the Romans hardening their hearts that they may remain in their abominations, the Jews of Asia Minor travestying his words lest they may be converted, that his tears of sorrow turn to tears of indignation, and he denounces them for their falsehood of heart. And in later times, when we get at the soul of St. Francis Xavier, we find that the sword which has pierced it is not the enormous sacrifice he has made, not the burden of his labors, not even the disappointments he meets with among his followers, but the fact that so many, Europeans and Indians alike, will not listen to that which in their hearts they know to be the truth.

The ways of this perversity are easily discovered by one who sees beneath the surface;

only to those whose standard and kingdom are "of this world" do they appear upright and worthy. For "this world" has indeed a standard of its own; there are many virtues of which it approves. It approves of the virtue of honesty; it makes much of the virtue of justice; it praises the "broad and open mind," which can see good in every form of doctrine, which is tolerant to all, which offers its understanding sympathy to every side.

But one thing "this world" will not tolerate; it will not endure interference with itself. Let truth be theoretical and no more, and it will be welcome; let it "go about doing good" and it will be encouraged; but let the suspicion once be raised that truth is aggressive, that it has set out to conquer as well as to serve, that the heart of the individual man is not secure against its invasions, and at once the tone is altered. Truth, hitherto a welcome friend, is now passed by and evaded; the search after truth, hitherto a delightful task, is now ignored as alien; sympathy with truth, and with the struggle and work of truth, is no longer, is now set aside with a query; it is no concern of ours, let truth look to itself, let those look to it to whom it belongs, its kingdom and ours are different.

Still there is a splendid dignity which, if possible, "this world" will never set aside. It is master of its own domain; as a master it will always rule. Others may be votaries and enemies of truth; "this world," with set chin and unflinching eye, endeavors to keep the peace between them. It may be that to preserve this peace, one side or the other must be treated severely; more severely, perhaps, than it deserves; perhaps even there may be downright injustice. Still "this world" goes through it all with that formal show of dispassionate independence which alone becomes it as a gentleman; even if in the end truth is to be condemned, however manifestly stainless, "this world" washes its hands before all, declares its innocence of guilt, lays the responsibility on those who have forced its hands, and leaves discarded truth to its fate, while itself remains upon its throne of "Justice."

Jesus Christ stood before Pilate; a Roman master to whom Judaism meant no more than a curious thing among the many curiosities of the East. To him the Jews were men and no more, subject for the time to his dominion; Jesus Christ was a man and no more, to be defended and released. To the Jews this Pilate was one who stood upon his dignity, to whom this dignity was especially dear, to whom religious differences mattered little, but who might be affected by charges of public disorder.

With solemnity, therefore, and with a demon-
stration of coolness, and of justice, and perhaps
of contempt for these Eastern fanatics, does this
judge open the trial: "What accusation bring
you against this man?" But these Eastern fanatics know well how to take him; he is far more
at their mercy than he is aware. To bring
forward the real charge before such a man, at
first at least, would be useless; for religion he
had too profound a contempt to put a man to
death on its account. Some other charges must
be tried, something that would more appeal to
a man of the world; something above all that
shall seem to affect him and his honor.

So does the accusation turn. "If he were not
a malefactor, we would not have delivered him to
thee." But this charge is too general, and Pilate
can treat it with contempt; he can leave it to
them to decide. Then another step is taken.
"We have found this man perverting our nation.
He stirreth up the people, teaching throughout
Judea, beginning from Galilee to this place."
Still can Pilate avoid passing sentence; he can
hand the case over to the Galilæan Herod. They
must strike nearer home. "We have found this
man forbidding to give tribute to Cæsar, and
saying he is the Christ the King."

Now they have reached their first goal; Pilate
contemptuous is at least made interested. He

will examine this Jesus Christ for himself; he
will be fair to both sides, there may be something in the last accusation which it would be
well for him to know. He has heard of this
"King of the Jews" before; he may now find
an opportunity of learning more.

"Art thou the man known as the King of the
Jews?" he asks his Prisoner. But Jesus Christ
knows that to give an immediate answer to this
uninstructed heathen is useless; he must first
be taught the meaning of the phrase he has
used. Does Pilate really wish to know, does he
really seek for instruction for himself, or is he
only curious? At once the man of the world is
on his guard. Instruction for himself? Is he
a Jew? What can he personally care? He was
merely there to administer justice; what had
the Prisoner done?

But truth is not so easily silenced; at least
it will tell this man enough of the kingdom to
put him at his ease if he had any doubts. For
the kingdom was not of this world; neither Jews
nor Romans need have any fear of opposition.
But a King He was; for this was He born, and
for this He came into the world, that He might
testify to the truth; and everyone that sincerely
sought the truth would listen.

This was the crucial moment. Hitherto the
man of the world had been interested, even

sympathetic, determined to save this innocent victim. But there was something about Him that was suspicious; there was authority in His voice, dignity in His manner, aggressiveness in His defense of "truth." Already he had felt the attraction; perhaps already he had shown himself too affected; if he submitted to much more he might find himself awkwardly involved. It would be better to know no more.

"Truth? What is truth?" he asked; and before an answer could be given he had turned upon his heel. He had been given the choice of two services, and the choice was made. Henceforth he might make some further effort to be externally fair and just. He might declare the Prisoner's guiltlessness; he might affect indignation that Jesus Christ would not defend Himself; he might yield a little that the main point might be gained; he might make more show than ever of an effort to be just and honorable; but the die had been cast, he had made his choice, and the enemy knew well how he could be bent to its purpose. He had wavered on the point of the kingship; then this should be driven deeper home. Therefore the cry is howled out: "If thou release this man, thou art not Cæsar's friend; for whosoever maketh himself a king speaketh against Cæsar."

Poor perverse Pontius Pilate! He would still

play the gentleman; still would he show his contempt for this uncontrolled mob; but he had refused the opportunity, he "would not" when he could have chosen, and while he affected indifference and justice, cruelty after cruelty fell upon the Man whom he pretended to defend; while he held the outward bearing of strength, no man in the story of the Passion stands convicted of so much cowardice.

But such by nature is "the world." It has a bold front enough. It knows its external duties. It will live up to its standard along its own lines. But ask it for realities, ask it to face the truth that is not welcome, and there is no tyrant can be so cruel, so utterly unjust—yes, at times, even on its own confession—as this otherwise temperate, self-controlled, discriminating world.

THE JUDGMENT OF JUDAS

"There is a friend that turneth to enmity; and there is a friend that will disclose hatred and strife and reproaches."—Eccles. vi. 10.

HE was more than what might be called one of the general body of the apostles. He was one specially gifted; perhaps, from man's point of view, the most promising of all. Alone of the twelve he came from Judæa, while most of the rest were merely Galilæans; he stood evidently above them all in his experience of the world, for it was decided that he should manage their money, and when he spoke he showed marked sagacity and human prudence. And his life had corresponded to this judgment of him; he had always lived in keeping with his rank as "one of the twelve"; when they were told that one among them was to be a traitor, none of them, even after all these years of intercourse, could have guessed that it would be he; and when they did hear the truth they were struck with amazement.

Yet this was the man. He had entered on his life with eagerness and zeal, he had followed his Master everywhere; in his enthusiastic fervor he had said that nothing should ever separate them. Yet time had told; in his Master he had been a little disappointed, for he had discovered that He was "only Jesus" after all; he had been even more disappointed in the kingdom, for he had seen, even quicker than the others, that it was "not of this world"; most of all he had been disappointed in regard to himself, for he had understood that the kingdom was to belong to the poor in spirit, and by those who suffered persecution. Long ago he had made up his mind what he wanted, and it was nothing of this kind. What it was he had pictured to himself does not matter; it was not this, and that was enough.

He was disillusioned; he was not to have what he looked for, he, the sagacious, the prudent, the wise, found himself in the wrong after all. His heart grew more bitter, his mind more clouded, his faith in his Master more doubtful, in himself more secure. And precisely there the conflict came; he must choose between his Master and himself, he must be faithful to Him and give up his own way, or have his own way and be faithless. And gradually the second conquered; self-will, self-satisfaction won, and the

114

rest was but a matter of time. First dissatisfaction, then seemingly justifiable complaint, then plotting, and finally the worst of all.

He is there in the Garden; he kisses his Master; and he hears the complaint:

"Judas, you whom I have chosen from the beginning, you whom I have made my own and have loved in a special manner as my very own, you whom I have trusted even more than the others by giving you the care of the purse, you whom this trust has brought into more frequent intercourse with me, you to whom I have given the power of working miracles, you whom I have sent out with the rest to preach my word, my chosen representative, my appointed ambassador, you whose feet I have washed, you whose heart I have read and told you clearly that I read it, whom I have never thrown away though I knew your growing faithlessness, whom I have never betrayed to others though I knew you unworthy of their company, you who brazened out your treachery by open falsehood, who abused me and mine under the pretense of piety and zeal for the poor, you to whom I gave all I had, to whom I have given my very self, my own body and my blood, you into whose hands I have trusted my good name, my honor, my heart, you whom alone posterity shall know that I have called 'Friend'—

"Friend Judas, do you of all men betray me? Do you prefer your own satisfaction to my love, to my honor, to my very life? Do you still pretend one thing to me and all the time are so different? Do you presume upon this very friendship and trust, knowing you are trusted, and that I will not expose you before men, no matter what you may do, and therefore knowing that you can play me false with impunity? Of all men do you betray me, and in such a shameful manner? Do you betray me with a kiss, and bid me 'Hail!' and call me 'Master,' as if your heart were rejoiced at meeting me?

"You kiss me, and tell me you love me, and you know that I will accept your word, and therefore, and by that means, you betray me? Oh! Judas, there are many ways in which you can hurt a friend, but none is more cruel than this. You might have given up if you had liked, you might have openly turned against me, you might have declared me a deceiver of men; but you need not have done this. You take me for your friend, I take you for mine, and we have sealed our friendship by many sacred pledges; you have said all yours is mine, I have said all mine is yours and I have proved it; and now that we have made that compact, and friendship has tied my hands, and I have trusted you with

116

my whole self, you take this very means, and
seal it with a kiss, to betray me!

"Soon, in an hour or two, you will repent of
what you do; nay, at this very moment do you
not despise yourself for doing it? With all your
show of peace and quiet, in spite of all your
company at your back, are you not beset with
abject fear lest after all your new friends should
realize what you do, should see through your
treachery, should despise you and spurn you even
while they use you for their tool? But soon it
will be far worse. When my warning voice is
silenced, when men have become too engrossed
to notice you, when you are left alone with
yourself and your thirty silver coins, then you
will know in your heart what you have done.
You will hate yourself, you will contemn yourself, you will despair at the thought that you
are what you are, you will hang yourself in your
misery, and for all time to come your very name
will be a by-word for all that is base in human
nature. And all this because you kiss me as a
friend, being all the time a traitor; you kiss
me as a devoted son, being only a crafty self-
seeker; you kiss me as one of mine, being
already sold to my enemies; you kiss me because
you know I love you, because you know I trust
you, and all the time your own love is dead,
and trust has become your cloak for treachery."

So did the Heart of Jesus feel, whatever it may have said, when Judas betrayed Him with a kiss; so, or at least in part it was so, for behind the deed of human treachery, behind the offense against Himself as man, there was the offense against Himself as God, of which He could no longer speak to such a man as Judas. For "Satan had entered into him," and his heart was hardened to do malice; as must be the heart of many a man before it can be brought to do its final deed.

"Yes," his heart replies, "I know that what I do is basely evil and a deed of everlasting shame. I know I am a traitor, fit only for contempt and execration. I know I have received more than others. I have been chosen by this Jesus Christ, and have responded to His choice. I have been brought into close union with Him, and have come to know Him more openly than all the rest, and have lived an outward life in accordance with that office. I have fed at His table. I have been trained by His own word and His companionship. I have from Him only friendship, and kindness, and indulgence. I have learned from Him what are the depths of love, and how to love, both from the love that He has poured on me, and from the love He has stirred in my own heart.

118

"I know I shall be sorry for the deed I do. I know I shall break His heart; and I know that the injustice I commit, the shame I incur, will be nothing in comparison with this. I know I shall break the hearts of others, who believe in me, and love me, and trust me, and build their hopes upon me; who have not yet discovered the malice that is in me, and would not believe it even if they were told. I know I shall break my own heart, such as there is left of it; I shall be dead to all shame, dead to all human feeling, a dead soul in a living body, that may even seek relief in destroying what life remains.

"But I do not care. I will have my way. I will indulge my passion. I choose to do this hideous deed and I will do it, come what come may. I will satisfy myself. I will defy God, and man, and my very self. I will shut my eyes to every consequence. Nay, if need be, I will sin, and sin, and sin again, that my heart may be hardened, that my eyes may be blinded, that all hope of return may be closed. I will take vengeance on Him for loving me so much. That I may make Him suffer the more, I will destroy the best that is in myself. I will betray innocent blood. I will listen to no reason, no appeal; I will, and that shall be enough."

How perverse, we say, how brutally cruel! And yet, when any grave sin is unmasked, when

the excuses are removed and the specious pre-
texts set aside, when the truth is laid bare and
the secret motives of the soul are revealed, how
often is this but its description! "I know I am
doing wrong, but I will do it. I know I do myself
lasting injury, but I do not care. I know the
injustice, the cruelty, I inflict on others, even
on Jesus Christ Himself, but I will have my
way." So says the sinner in his heart; and in
proportion to his deliberation in saying it is the
depth of the evil he commits. Is it wonderful
that a certain saint, who knew well what was in
man, tells us that the secret of sin is self-will,
that the secret of uprightness is self-conquest?

THE JUDGMENT OF THE PEOPLE

"How long will this people detract me? How long will they not believe me for all the signs that I have wrought before them?"—Num. xiv. 11.

THE Jews were indeed the chosen people; but it will hardly be claimed by anyone that they were always a very faithful people. The history of the Old Testament is little more than a record of the favors and promises the Hebrews received from their God, of their weariness in and rejection of His allegiance, of their punishment and consequent repentance; and of their reception once more into His favor and affection. The wandering in the Desert, Sodom and Gomorrha, Saul, David, Elias, Isaias, Jeremias—what do all these and many more names recall but a repeated tale of promise, and failure, and punishment, and ultimate forgiveness?

But it is important to remember that forgiveness did not come in the end. Much as the Sacred Text voices the anger of God with His faithless children, still there is no mistaking the tenderness of that very anger, the appeal that His hand may be stayed even while it is raised to strike, the promise of forgiveness alongside of the threat of punishment; the waiting and waiting before the final blow descends. Abraham, Joseph, Moses, Samson, Nathan, and all the prophets—these and many more are witness to the God of forgiveness, whose mercy is above all His works, who willeth the death of none, but rather that all should be converted and live.

When we come to the New Testament the story is the same. "Seeing the multudes he had compassion on them: because they were distressed, and lying like sheep that have no shepherd." This is the text that sums up the attitude of Jesus Christ towards the poor, misled people about Him. "He came unto his own, and his own received him not. But to as many as did receive him to them he gave the power to become the sons of God." His life is a story of continuous disappointments; of high expectations ending in nothing, of individual desires and ambitions quaking at the prospect of sacrifice and too often failing in the end; and yet withal there is alongside the inexhaustible abyss of His mercy, waiting for the return of each, continually inviting all to come, appealing by look and word and action, seeing only the possibilities for good in these wayward and disloyal crowds. He dwells seldom on Himself as the Almighty Judge, and then only by way of solemn warning; much more does He prefer to call Himself the Bread of Life, the Good Shepherd, the Way to the Father, the Lover of men, the Meek and Humble of heart who, when lifted up, will draw all things to Himself.

In spite, then, of every provocation, and in spite of occasional denunciations, there is no mistaking the love which Jesus Christ bore towards His own people; even His very denunciations are expressed in terms of love and break down in tears of affection. Listen to the strongest of them all: "Jerusalem, Jerusalem, that killest the prophets, and stonest them that are sent to thee, how often would I have gathered thy children as the bird doth her brood under her wings, and thou wouldst not? Behold your house shall be left to you desolate. And I say to you, that you shall not see me till the time come, when you shall say, Blessed is he that cometh in the name of the Lord." From beginning to end the love of Jesus Christ for the crowds about Him never wavered; with them He never lost patience, no matter what they did.

And it is easily understood. For what is any crowd but a mass of ignorance, wandering in the dark and in confusion, made weaker by its very strength, since the greater its number the greater must be the babel of tongues to which it is compelled to listen? What is it but a huge dependent force, unable to act for itself by the very independence of its units, dependent on any power that can master it, and by it led one way or another, little enough by any choice of its own, entirely, or almost entirely, under the sway of him that dominates it? Now it will cry its hosannas, hailing the coming of its hero; in another day it will look on him with suspicion, and denounce him as one who is no friend. At one time it will be lavish in its honors; at another the hungriest tiger cannot be so merciless and cruel. Today it will rush to death with the bravery of utter selflessness; tomorrow it will show cowardice and timidity that will shame human nature. Mastered by impulse and stirred-up passion, victim of every breath that blows upon it, doing deeds for which no human being would care to be responsible—there is something weird, sometimes diabolic, that will work on man when gathered in a mob.

But there is also the other side; Jesus Christ drew the attention of His disciples to it when He told them the parable of the Wheat and the Cockle. The wheat had been sown on the land that had been tilled, and both land and wheat were good. But cockle was sown by an enemy, and both wheat and cockle grew together. Still the wheat prevailed; there was a harvest after all; and He gave them to understand that in the midst of and in spite of all its disappointments, its fickleness and wickedness, and all its cruelties, at bottom human nature is good, and will bear its good fruit in season. Even the mob is made up of human beings; even these human beings, however tiger-like they may act here and now, have human hearts within them; and the time will come, when the chain that binds the crowd will break, when these human individuals will awaken from their madness, when they will realize what they have done, when they will turn away beating their breasts, in shame, in confusion, in sorrow, in amendment.

Jesus Christ stood before His people to be judged. Annas had rejected Him with contempt, and he had received little else in return. Caiphas had found religious grounds on which to condemn Him, and had heard in response the most solemn of warnings. Herod would have made Him a fool before the world, and he was within a very little of being himself befooled. Pilate paraded as the minister of justice; no man has ever done greater injustice in its name. And now was the turn of the people to pass sentence. With them there is no posing, no pretense, scarcely even any plea of reason; it is all mad frenzy from first to last. He is a malefactor, this Man of whom they had said: "Behold he hath done all things well; he hath made the deaf to hear and the dumb to speak." He is a seducer, this Man whom they had hailed for His utter truthfulness. He desired to make Himself a king, this Man who had more than once escaped their hands because a king He would not be.

Reckless, contradictory, confused, shameless, the mob hurled out its accusations. But its deeds were worse than its cries; deeds at once the height of cruelty and cowardice. It began in the Garden when without any provocation they "seized and bound him like a thief"; it was continued on the road to Annas; it reached its first climax when the blow on the face in the house of the high-priest was greeted with approval. The example was set them for further atrocities by the spitting and abuse of the Scribes and Pharisees; when next morning He was dragged before Pilate, and to and from the court of Herod, it is terrible to think what He must have endured at the hands of this tiger-hearted rabble. He was scourged, that they might see His blood flow down, and it did but whet their appetite for more; crowned with thorns, and they were not satisfied; exposed to them in all His shame and ignominy, "a worm and no man," and they only cried out the more: "Crucify him, crucify him, let him be crucified!" And, when nothing else seemed likely to prevail, then with the hoarse yell of reckless passion they invoked the curse upon themselves: "His blood be upon us and upon our children!"

Surely this was enough. They had been more merciless than any other of His judges; surely now He would condemn. And yet no; He had defended them before in His lifetime, when they had mocked Him on the roadside, and the indignant disciples had asked Him to call down fire from heaven; and He would not punish them now. He had always been tender with them, even when He had been most severe; and He would not be different now. For He "knew what was in man"; He "knew their dust"; He saw them "as sheep without a shepherd"; and even in that dread hour His heart of compassion went out to them. He had come "for the lost sheep of the house of Israel," and no matter how they treated Him He would "love them to the end." In the midst of all the cruelty, yes, even at its worst, still did the prayer rise up to His Father: "Father, forgive them, for they know not what they do."

And His prayer was heard. When this mob had done its worst, when He was dead and they had before them the fruit of their labors, then the spell was broken, and passion, as always, was followed at once by remorse, and each man came in conflict with his own conscience, and they held down their heads, and turned away their eyes, and "went back to the city beating their breasts"; and fifty days later, when they were told in plain words what they had done, there were numbers, great numbers among them who accepted once again Him whom they had done to death.

With the multitude Jesus was not angry; He had for them only pity. But upon those who led them astray, for them He had only indignation. "It must needs be that scandal should come; but woe to that man by whom the scandal cometh."

THE JUDGMENT OF GOD

"Jesus Christ, who knew no sin, God hath made sin for us, that we might be made the justice of God in him."—2 Cor. v. 21.

WE may read in our morning paper of some atrocious crime that has been committed. The criminal has been captured; his name means nothing to us; in consequence almost our only feeling is of anger, and of hope that he will receive the punishment he deserves. But in the course of the day we discover we know something of the man. We may remember that we have met him; that his birth and upbringing have been wholly against him; that he has always been a victim of an uncontrollable temper, but is a good man at heart; that he depends very much on his surroundings; that he is very ignorant and has done many things he would not have done had he known better; and at once our indignation is modified, our anger is softened by pity, our demand for justice is tempered by mercy, and we are not so keen as we were that the criminal should be visited with the full rigor of the law.

We may go yet farther. In a day or two it may be discovered that this man was not the guilty one at all. Another is taken, and his name is exposed. We know this name, perhaps only too well. He may be a kinsman, however distant, of our own; he may have the same name as ourselves. He may have been an intimate acquaintance, of whom we have always thought well. He may even now be one of those whom we have considered as belonging to our inner circle of friends. At once our whole attitude is altered. It is not anger that is first aroused, but a sense of horror; not so much pity, but sympathy and feeling; not a desire that justice in the first sense should be satisfied, but that every preliminary reason should be produced, every fact should be mustered, every extenuating circumstance should be set in order, to show that this man could not have done such a deed, or did not do it, or, if he did it, was in some way wholly irresponsible, or, last of all, if there is no other escape, deserves that his crime should be punished in some other way. Nay, our love for the man, and our belief in the man, may be such that if he is condemned we may feel that we would gladly bear the punishment in his stead;

and many a time has love and true friendship
led to this act of heroism.

Thus in our human judgments we understand
how great a difference is made by a very little
thing. In all three cases it may be said that
none is more just, nor less just, than another;
and yet how different, even how opposite, are
the goals to which justice works and the methods
by which it proceeds! Of the three, rigid justice
may well be the greatest injustice; justice tempered by understanding pity may be more true;
justice kindled by love may be transformed, and,
so long as justice remains at all, will be the
truest of all.

When men speak of God, and the anger of
God, and the justice of God, they usually forget
the inadequacy of the words they use. We,
creeping human beings have only human language at our command; and if this is incapable
of expressing even human ideas, how much less
can human words express the idea of God! If,
for example, as we have just seen, the simple
word justice, in itself so easily defined, so clear-
cut and concise, may nevertheless mean three
totally different things according to the persons
to whom it is applied, how much less will it
accurately contain all the truth when it is applied to God! Justice in man may be always so
varied, and yet remain always justice; justice

in God is many things at once, and yet is always itself. In truth the justice of God is the mercy of God! His mercy is His love; His love is once again His justice; and it is only by blending them all together, and treating none apart from the rest, that we can form any true idea of what is meant by His wrath and His forgiveness.

Man has done evil in the sight of God; justice requires that this evil should in some way be atoned; until that evil is atoned, it is right to speak of the wrath and anger of an offended God, even in the vehement language of the ancient prophets. But man is a creature of God; man in himself is a very feeble creature; man in his circumstances is a creature that can scarcely save itself from evil-doing. Hence to know man is to pity him; though justice may demand his punishment, yet pity would have it tempered with mercy; and God who "knows our dust," even more than we know it ourselves, looks on man with eyes of pity as well as with eyes of wrath, works to satisfy the demands of mercy even while the dictate of justice is no less satisfied.

But God is more than understanding, and man is more than a feeble creature crawling upon this earth. God is the Maker of man, and He has more than a passing interest in the work of His hands. God is the Father of man, the author of his life, and man is the child of God in every real sense. God is the Friend and Lover of man, and even "to the end," whatever his vagaries, man is God's beloved. More, then, than mercy tempers the justice of God. Man may sin, but the love of God goes out to His wayward child. He may be wilful, and reckless, and offensive; but the love of the father's heart, even of the mother's pleading, the true affection of the friend and lover, pleads with offended justice, and God entreats with God, not merely that pity and mercy may be shown, but that atonement may be made, in some other way; yes, even, if so it can be, that God Himself may atone to Himself for the evil that is done and that man may be suffered to go free.

When, then, the Father looks upon the Son nailed and dead upon the Cross, the judgment goes out, as it had gone out before: "This is My beloved Son, who has seen My justice offended by man, who has seen that man, capable of offending, is nevertheless unable to atone; who has therefore Himself become man, identified Himself with man, "hath been made sin for man," that so justice may be fully satisfied. This is My beloved Son, who has seen My pity for man, who has seen that man is incapable of responding to that pity, who has therefore taken on Himself the life of man, that so He might

lift man up to the life divine. This is My beloved
Son, who has known My love for man, who has
loved man with My own love, who has been led
by love to plead for man, to point to all the good
that is in man, to give Himself that man might
escape, to lay aside for man His very Godhead,
so far as that could be, to take up man's whole
manhood, to be born for man, to live for man,
to die for man, "quickening man together with
himself; forgiving all man's offenses; blotting
out the handwriting of the decree that was
against him; taking the same out of the way,
fastening it to the cross." This is My beloved
Son who has satisfied justice, for man has now
atoned for man; who has satisfied mercy, for
man has received condonement; who has satisfied
love, for love knows no limits, love gives all, and
love has prompted Him to stop at nothing; not
at the surrender of heaven, not at the Incarna-
tion, not at the journey of His life, not until,
here on Calvary, with the last drop of His human
blood poured out, there was absolutely nothing
else to give. "This is my beloved Son, in whom
I am well pleased."

This is the judgment of God upon Jesus
Christ crucified. Man has done his worst; the
sun has hidden itself in shame at the spectacle;
but through the gloom the Cross shines out, the
signal at once of defeat and of triumph. Man

has sinned; man is crucified; and those who understand rush to that cross, and place their hands upon His hands, and their feet upon His feet, and cry out in joy with St. Paul: "With Christ I am nailed to the cross." For dying with Him they know that with Him they rise; only the "old man" remains on the wood "crucified." "Therefore," concludes St. Paul, "if you be risen with Christ, seek the things that are above, where Christ is sitting at the right hand of God. Mind the things that are above, not the things that are upon the earth. For you are dead; and your life is hid with Christ in God."

The pen drops from the fingers in despair when one endeavors to express in words the meaning of the Cross of Jesus Christ; the meaning as it is contained in the judgment of "God the Father of our Lord Jesus Christ," and the Father of all us men. We catch a glimmer of the truth; as we look in tears of bitterness and joy, the light grows upon us; only those who draw near, and place their hearts beneath the dripping blood, and pierce their hands and heads with the nails and thorns, and let the world close round them in blackness and night, even the night of death, can hope to come to that perfect understanding which is the glory of the Lord, and the perfect joy of earth as well as of heaven. —Jesus Christ, the beginning and the end! "I

account myself as knowing nothing but Jesus
Christ and him crucified."—"From henceforth
let no man trouble me. For I bear the marks
of the Lord Jesus in my body."

WHAT THINK YOU OF CHRIST?

"WHAT after all, in practical life, does Jesus Christ mean to you?" I was asked the other day by an inquiring Hindu. What does He mean to me? The answer is so vast that I wonder how and where I shall begin. As St. John tells us, if we were to write down all that Jesus Christ is to us, "the world, I think, would not contain the books that must be written." What is He to me? He is Alpha and Omega; He is first and last; He is the beginning and the end. He is before all else, He is after every other; in Him, and from Him, and with Him, and for Him are all things; to Him for ever and ever be all the glory that any being can win for Him; that is enough to make up the sum and substance of my life.

What does He mean to me? There was a day when my hungry little heart came groping into this world, looking for it knew not what, grasping by turns at this thing and that and the other, fascinated in successive hours by the ever new horizon of life, yet for ever falling back to its initial wondering, and disillusionment, and unrest. Life to it then was the opening of a ball; and oh! what a dance and a revel it would be! There might be light and darkness, there would be days of trouble and days of toil, possibly there might come suffering and sorrow, but there was the nimbleness of springtime in the childish feet, the whiteness of the snowdrop in the heart, the laughter of the morning sunshine in the eyes, which looked to the future undismayed, ambitious for the best, confident, keen, holding all the world as but a merry hunting-ground.

But it wanted a companion, though it scarcely knew the fact itself; hungry as it was, that laughing little heart could not live long alone. And here came its first disappointment, its first lesson in disillusion. It cleaved to another heart, the same size as its own, and death came and took it away. It went about its tiny world, carrying its love upon its sleeve, saying: "Who will have it?" And some others just sipped and tasted, and others accepted a little; but the hungry little heart only wondered the more that the world with all its contents could after all be so empty, so hollow.

Until one day it seemed to awaken. It had

been looking the wrong way, looking too far afield; the satisfaction of its hunger was within its grasp all the time. All the time it had, and had always had, a companion; a baby in its babyhood, a child in its childhood, a youth beside its youth, a man keeping pace with its manhood; happy when it was happy, sorrowing when it was sorrowful, when it was triumphant sharing in its triumph; no more than itself and yet enclosing and embracing it, accepting all the love that it was capable of giving and giving so much more in return; hungering more than it hungered, and putting its hunger to shame; so that from henceforth that tiny little heart forgot its own hunger in its longing to satisfy this other hungry heart whose cravings mattered so much more.

What is Jesus Christ to me? "Christ loved me and gave himself to me and for me"; that is what He means to me. Christ loved me, and asked me for my love; that is what He means to me. Christ loved me, and came down the lane of life looking for me, and became a child with me, and exchanged His confidences with me, and listened while I told Him my heart's desire, and told me His heart's desire in return, and gave Himself to me, and taught me how to love in a way I had never known before, nor could anyone else have taught me. Christ loved me, and let me see a little of His Heart; and I felt its trembling weakness yet leaned upon its strength; I pitied its littleness yet gloried in its greatness; I ached for its sadness yet triumphed in its glory; all within me was a turmoil of joy and anguish, and when I turned to go away I found my heart had been stolen from me. He had stolen my heart from me, and it was an agony; but an agony so sweet that I trust to have it till my dying day.

What is Jesus Christ to me? Have you got your answer? Have you any idea of true love, or do you only know that limping counterfeit which most men take for the truth? Do you know what is love unsatisfied, fostered in loneliness and endurance, until it threatens to burst your craving heart? Do you know what it is to have this intolerable strain suddenly removed, the void suddenly filled up, to have "found Him whom your soul loveth, to have held Him and not to let Him go"? If you do not, then you cannot have even the least idea of what Jesus Christ means to me, and to every Christian who possesses Him, and you never can. Do you know what it is to have your love as it were reversed, so that no longer do you desire to find it satisfied but rather you crave to satisfy with all your life the love of another? Do you know what it is so to love that you forget your own existence in the loving, that you are ashamed to confound pleasure with love, that the only delight in love is to suffer, that your life now becomes but a longing to give, and to endure, and to toil? If you do not, then you cannot understand what Jesus Christ is to me, and to us Christians, and you never can.

But if you do know even a little of these things, if your heart is still human, if your love is not yet dead, then you may at least begin to know. You may come to recognize this Lord and Friend of mine, who is no more than I am and yet is infinite in all perfections, who is really on my level and yet is very God of heaven and earth, who rejoices to live in my cottage and yet all creation cannot contain Him, who is "the Lord" and yet "only Jesus," who knows my limitations yet loves me with an everlasting love. You may know what He is to me, who will never leave me no matter how low down I may go, who will never see me suffer but He must suffer alongside, who will never have a joy or a sorrow of His own but He will ask me to share it.

His proof of love takes my breath away and I cannot speak; His condescension almost makes me doubt; so human is He that many even of His friends will not believe it is all true. They say He is God; and they will not feel His throbbing Heart beside their own. They say He is too far away, and they will not believe that His bleeding hand lies between theirs. They say He is too great to need a love like theirs, too perfect for a sinful soul like theirs, too almighty, too faultless, to need their comfort, and they will not see the price He has paid, the self He has annihilated, the eyes welling with hot tears, that He might be wholly one with them, that He might both give human love and receive it.

What is Jesus Christ to me? He is my love in the deepest human sense of which my human heart is capable; do I need to say any more? He is my satisfaction, pressed down deep and flowing over, is not that enough? He is my inspiration: in Him, and for Him, and from Him, and with Him is my life and all that it contains: let Him take it and do with it exactly what He pleases. He is my strength and my support; when I fail He lifts me up, when I suffer He is my companion, when I am alone and despairing, He is at my side. And He is my crown; I ask for nothing more; with Him, come what may, I know I shall have enough, here in this life and for all eternity.

Much more than this is Jesus Christ to me; but for the moment let this be enough. His love has transformed mine; not crushed it but enlarged it; it has given me another power of loving; whereas before I looked for but one,

now I know that my heart has expanded, and
while it loves the one none the less, there is
room in it for the love of all the world beside.
But that will take me too far afield: it is enough
that I have touched on just the essential of what
Jesus Christ is to me; in other words of what
it is to be a Christian, for what He is to me
He is to everyone in his degree. That is the
wonder of it: while He loves you, He loves me
no less, while He loves you and me with all the
love we creatures can receive, He loves all the
world with an infinite love. Let a man learn that
and it will suffice; but love Jesus Christ and
you will discover all the rest. You will learn in
very truth what love means; not the cramped,
limping, narrowed, self-indulgent thing that men
often fancy it, but the great, noble, self-sacrific-
ing, all-embracing thing that makes a man close
akin to the loving God Himself.

GRAIL PAMPHLETS

A MORE EXCELLENT WAY .... 10¢
  by Archbishop Goodier, S.J.
CAROLS FOR CHRISTMAS .... 25¢
  by Mary Fabyan Windeatt
CHRIST AND THE SOUL .... 10¢
  Examination of Conscience for Religious
CHRIST CALLS .... 25¢
  by Theodore Heck, O.S.B., Ph.D.
COME AND SEE .... 25¢
  by Benedictine Monks
COMPLINE .... 10¢
  according to the Monastic Breviary
DIGEST OF THE LITURGICAL SEASONS 25¢
  by Bernard Beck, O.S.B.
DOVE FLIGHTS .... 25¢
  by Benedictine Sisters
EUCHARISTIC CHRIST .... 10¢
  by Placidus Kempf, O.S.B.
FLYING HIGH .... 25¢
  by James M. Darby, S.M.
FOLLOW CHRIST, Vocation Booklet .... 25¢
  published annually
FRUITFUL DAYS .... 25¢
  by Placidus Kempf, O.S.B.
GLORIES OF DIVINE GRACE .... 25¢
  by Matthias Scheeben
GOSPEL MOVIES SERIES
  by Placidus Kempf, O.S.B.
  (1) Grace .... 10¢
  (2) Faith .... 10¢
  (3) Sins .... 10¢
  (4) Wed in Christ .... 10¢